CRESCENTA VALLEY PIONEERS & THEIR LEGACIES

JO ANNE SADLER

Published by The History Press
Charleston, SC 29403
www.historypress.net

First published 2012

Manufactured in the United States

ISBN 978.1.60949.562.6

Library of Congress CIP data applied for.

Notice: The information in this book is true and complete to the best of our knowledge. It is offered without guarantee on the part of the author or The History Press. The author and The History Press disclaim all liability in connection with the use of this book.

Contents

Acknowledgements

Thanks to all the unnamed people whose interest in family history has helped me in my endeavors over the past thirty years. Thank you to Melissa Patton, director, and Tim Gregory, archivist, at the Lanterman Historical Museum Foundation for their generous sharing of materials and photographs that greatly enhanced this book.

Thanks to all libraries, but especially to the Glendale Public Library and its Special Collections Room, the Los Angeles Public Library, the La Cañada Flintridge Public Library and the Southern California Genealogical Society Library and their extensive collections and publications. Thanks to Dr. Peter J. Blodgett and Bill Frank at the Huntington Library Archives for their assistance and to the Huntington Library for saving and archiving nineteenth-century Los Angeles County Vital and Court Records.

Among the descendants of valley pioneers who have generously shared photographs and information about their families, I thank Jacqueline Kennedy, Lori Ward Kent, James McHargue, Bill Mann, L.K. Shackelford and Richard W. Williams.

And finally, this book would not have been written without the recommendation, encouragement and support of Mike Lawler, president of the Historical Society of the Crescenta Valley. He has greatly helped revitalize interest in Crescenta Valley history.

Unless otherwise noted, photographs and graphics in this book are from the archives of the Historical Society of the Crescenta Valley.

Introduction

The current Crescenta Valley encompasses the communities of La Cañada Flintridge, Glendale Annex, La Crescenta and Montrose. The area was part of the Mexican land grant Rancho La Cañada that was carved out of a larger Spanish land grant, Rancho San Rafael, and federal land north of the rancho. The valley is located at the base of the San Gabriel Mountains running from the Arroyo Seco to the Sunland/Tujunga border. The Tongva Indians were the original inhabitants; permanent villages have been found in neighboring Sunland/Tujunga, but none has been found in the Crescenta Valley. It is believed the Tongva used the area on a seasonal basis for hunting and when the abundant canyon water was available. A Mission Trail was established from San Gabriel Mission to San Fernando Mission and ran along the base of the foothills.

With the arrival of the Spanish and the establishment of the mission system, the Tongva were pushed out and moved to the San Gabriel Mission. They were gone from the area by the early 1800s. After the American Civil War, the great westward expansion brought more and more eastern pioneers to California. Many were Civil War veterans. Settlement of the Crescenta Valley began in the early 1870s.

Land north of the Rancho La Cañada property was federal, railroad and state school owned. None of the early settlers acquired their land under the 1862 Homestead Act. Instead, they acquired federal land under the Land Act of 1820, which allowed for the purchase of 160 acres for $2.50 per acre. Permanent residency had to be established and the property improved. The federal land was not yet surveyed, so the early settlers established residency on their properties under the right of preeminence with the intention to file land patent applications and secure the properties when the land was surveyed. These early settlers were called "squatters," which was not very nice, especially since they had to pay for part of the properties when they applied for the land patents. Usually, the process took six years. Once a property was deeded to a settler, it became private, and the government no longer had any control over the land.

While there were many subsequent people who have made major contributions to the development of the area, I am focusing on only the very first settlers, the first ones to "turn the soil," so to speak. As we drive around the Crescenta Valley, we see many street names, canyons, debris basins and landmarks, as well as historic structures, named for the original pioneers of the valley. But who were these people? They were not just names and dates but rather real people with full lives and experiences. Most were too busy making a living and surviving to sit down and write journals, so we must reconstruct their lives as best we can without romanticizing or vilifying them. Their lives were intertwined in both business and social spheres, so some of the narration may be repeated.

After joining the Historical Society of Crescenta Valley in 2009, I started doing research on the early pioneer settlers. What I found were many contradictory and varied stories. Many of the stories have been passed down for generations and/or related by people in their later years when the fog of memory does not always serve them well. Many stories were embellishments on the actual facts used to zip up the tales, and these contain many inaccuracies.

Credit must be given to June Doughtery in her 1993 *Sources of History La Crescenta* and Grace Oberbeck in her 1938 book, *History of La Crescenta–La Cañada Valleys*, because they did not perpetuate any of the negative, unsubstantiated stories. In the introduction to her book, Grace discusses her original hesitation about taking on the task of writing a history of the valley when approached by Mrs. Carpenter, publisher of the *Ledger*:

> *We informed her that we had no knowledge whatever of the facts concerning the Valley's early days. We had listened in on plenty of heresay and gossip, but surely that could not be given the high sounding name of history. Mrs. Carpenter assured us that was the proper frame of mind with which to approach the task. There would be no prejudices or former opinions to hamper us and we could write practically without emotion.*

This is the attitude I have taken in writing about Crescenta Valley history. My research is based on original legal records, land documents, memoirs, letters, newspaper articles and books of the day, with a little common sense thrown in.

Newspapers have been called the "first draft of history" and are extensively quoted. Newspapers, due to deadline constraints and conflicting witness statements, can contain errors, but many times they are the only witnesses we have to nineteenth-century events. What follows is what I have found about the lives of some of the earliest Crescenta Valley pioneers. Unlike many western immigrants who came because of lack of opportunity or economic necessity, many of the early pioneers came for the health benefits of the pure mountain air, with no frost or fogs, and to escape the harsh eastern winters. They have left their imprint on Crescenta Valley.

As for any errors or omissions, I offer a sincere mea culpa.

1

The Bathey Family

In 2009, after giving a presentation about the Bathey family at a meeting of the Historical Society of the Crescenta Valley, I received what I considered a left-handed compliment about my presentation, to the effect that I was able to bring some life to the "boring Batheys." Were the Batheys boring? I am sure they did not think so. The fact that they did not have any skeletons in the closet, were not horse thieves or involved in scandals, should not mean that they were not interesting people with purposeful lives.

Originally, the family name was Bathy, but the name later evolved into Bathey, so both names are shown as they appeared in the original records. The patriarch of the family was Charles Theodore Bathy, born in St. Clair County, Michigan, on March 28, 1850, the fourth child of Charles Theodore Bathy and Allie Waterloo. He had three brothers and two sisters. His younger brother George also came west and settled in Pasadena.

In 1870, Charles was living on the family farm but was farming his own land, which he acquired from the government under a land patent. He came to California about 1873, following his future wife, Mary Rebecca Goode, and her family. They were married on March 22, 1873, and had five children.

The Batheys lived in Los Angeles for at least ten years. Charles was a dairyman, builder and contractor. While there was no income tax at that time, people did pay different taxes and assessments, including head taxes and even taxes on beehives. In the 1881 "Assessment of the Property for

A surprise anniversary party given to Charles and Mary Bathey for their twenty-fifth wedding anniversary on March 22, 1898. *From left*: Winifred, Herbert, Roy (with dog), Charles, Mary, Edith and Allie.

Los Angeles City," Charles was assessed: "Hancock survey, subdivision lot 5 block 60, lots 1, 3, Block I; value of land $120; improvements $200. Total value of all property, $320; total tax $3.20; five percent, 16 cts. $3.83."

A $3.83 assessment doesn't seem like a lot, but it was about 1 percent of Charles's property value, which is roughly the same price we pay today for our property taxes. By 1884, he was registered to vote in Crescenta. His 1884 voter registration listed him as five-foot-nine, with a light complexion, gray eyes and brown hair. His occupation was farmer.

According to his land patent application, he first settled in La Crescenta in Section 22 on October 2, 1883, first camping out and then building a house. His witnesses to his application were Kirk W. Reynolds and George Engelhardt. His improvements included a house and fences. He broke land, kept bees and planted three acres with potatoes and vegetables. He also had a water tunnel. The land would not immediately provide a living for his family, and he undoubtedly lived in Los Angeles and La Crescenta at the same time. He later planted a fruit orchard from seeds his wife, Mary, obtained by mail order.

The Bathey house, circa 1900, built with stone terraces typical of the Crescenta Valley. Dogs were featured in many Bathey family pictures.

In 1890, the time for Bathey to file his final land patent papers was fast approaching when a Los Angeles real estate developer, Will D. Beach, filed an adverse claim on the property for timber rights. Beach claimed that Bathey did not live on the property full time, as was required. Bathey fought the accusation in court, filed his papers in time and retained the property, receiving his final land patent on May 13, 1890, for 151.49 acres.

Castle del Crescenta (Gould Castle)

Like all farmers, Bathey worked in the off-season in different occupations. He was the foreman for the construction of the Castle, also known as the Jerusalem Palace, Crescenta Palace, La Crescenta Castle and, as it is now commonly known, Gould Castle. Its building was commissioned by May I. Briggs Gould and her husband, Eugene W. Gould. May was the daughter of George Briggs, a pioneer fruit grower and one of California's first millionaires, as well as the brother of Dr. Benjamin B. Briggs. May had traveled to Europe with her parents and insisted (over Bathey's objections) on laying wood floors directly on the bare dirt, as this was the way it was done in Spain. The wood floors quickly deteriorated due to the moisture and were shortly pulled up and not replaced.

Gould Castle was commissioned by the niece of Dr. Benjamin B. Briggs, Mary Briggs Gould, and her husband, Eugene. It was abandoned in 1898, had several owners and was demolished in the 1950s. *Courtesy of Lori Ward Kent.*

Pierre Escalle, a local fruit grower and expert stonemason, worked under Bathey along with a gang of Chinese laborers. The Castle was built of local native granite quarried from the valley floor. After the Castle was built, Charles Bathey was hired in February 1894 to manage the estate and plant fruit and olive orchards; he worked and lived there for a year with his family. In May 1897, he sued the Goulds for $1,407.18 for back wages and expenses. He may have won the lawsuit, but by that time the Goulds were having financial problems, so it is doubtful he ever received the money.

A newspaper article reported that Bathey discovered the Castle abandoned by the Goulds in February 1898. Eugene Gould lost his fortune (and his wife's) in the raisin market. The Castle went through a succession of owners and was torn down in the 1950s.

Mary Rebecca Goode Bathey (Allie)

Mary was born in Rochester, New York, in May 1850 to Thomas Goode and Rebecca Abernathy, both born in Ireland. Her family moved to Los Angeles, and her future husband, Charles, followed her there. She was a founding member of the La Crescenta Presbyterian Church. The Bathey family was very close, and this reflects on the mother. Mary was undoubtedly devastated by the early death of her son Roy and died the following year of scrofula, or tuberculosis of the lymph nodes. She is buried in the family plot at Odd Fellows Cemetery in Los Angeles.

Working Hard

Son Herbert reflected on his father and said that a book could be written about him. He recounted a time before the Arroyo Seco Bridge had been built to get to Pasadena. When the Arroyo Seco was running after a winter rain, it was practically impossible to cross the stream. He remembered his dad driving a four-horse team across the river with a heavy load when the water was so high that wavelets rolled over the horses' backs. Charles Bathey was the epitome of what June Dougherty called "frontier hardened." He was not a gentleman farmer but a man with a large family to support and no safety net to fall back on. He did whatever he had to do to support his family.

In the orchard planted from seed that Mary Bathey requested from Washington, D.C. *From left*: Roy (seated with dog), Charles, Mary and possibly Winifred.

Herbert also said that the bandit Tiburcio Vasquez used to come to his father's dairy on Slauson in Los Angeles to buy cream and shoe his horses. This may be true, but Charles came to Los Angeles in 1873, and Vasquez was captured in 1874, so that is a short window for such interaction and was certainly before Herbert was born. After his wife died in 1904, Charles moved to Hollywood to live with Herbert, Winifred and Allie. He worked as a builder. He never remarried and died at California Hospital in Los Angeles on February 25, 1926, of complications from a perforated ulcer. He is buried in the family plot at Odd Fellows Cemetery.

Allie May Bathey

Charles and Mary's first child, Allie May, was born in Boyle Heights in April 1874. Along with her siblings Herbert and Winifred, Allie attended the elementary school at Los Angeles Normal School; all three are noted in the 1887 catalogue. This was a teacher's college located at Fifth and Hope Streets, the current site of the Los Angeles Central Library. This school was the predecessor of the University of California–Los Angeles (UCLA). In 1903, Allie was listed in her second year as a teaching student. There was no boarding at the school, but local families around the school took in student boarders. Allie was a public school teacher for thirty years specializing in manual training.

In the 1930 census, Allie was single, but by 1932 she had married John P. Johnson, and according to the voter registration, they were living with Winifred on Virginia Avenue in Hollywood. John soon disappeared from the record; what happened to him is not known. Allie went by Johnson for the rest of her life, but no husband was buried with her.

By 1948, Allie had retired and was living back at the Bathey ranch with her sister Winifred and brother Herbert. Herbert married in 1949 and moved away. Allie and Winifred held old-timers' reunions at the ranch, kept burros and raised bees. A great-grandson of Uncle George Bathey used to visit the ranch in the 1950s and '60s and remembered how nice Allie and Winifred were. He also fondly recalled the burros and always taking home a jar of honey and honeycomb. Allie died on September 7, 1964, and is buried in the family plot at Odd Fellows Cemetery in Los Angeles.

Winnie

Winifred was born in Boyle Heights on January 15, 1876. She attended school in Los Angeles, most likely boarding with a private family after her parents moved to La Crescenta. Winifred was artistic and attended the Los Angeles School of Art and Design located on Third and Spring Streets, Los Angeles. It was not affiliated with any other art school. On July 29, 1900, and again on September 21, 1901, Winfred was awarded a Certificate of Merit from the art school.

The president of the school was Dr. J.C. Fletcher, a Presbyterian minister. He was president from 1895 until his death in 1901. His extensive April 24, 1901 obituary states:

For the last six years, up to the time of death, Dr. Fletcher had been president of the Los Angeles School of Art and Design. While in Los Angeles where he had resided for the past ten years, he had been actively engaged in the ministry, but for the last two or three years had confined his attention especially to the little mission church at La Crescenta, where he was greatly loved, being an especial favorite of the children.

Dr. Fletcher most likely was the person who persuaded Winifred (and her parents to allow her) to attend the art school. It has been stated that Winifred graduated from USC Art School, but I find no record of this. Whether or not she studied under William Lees Judson, I cannot ascertain. Judson joined the faculty of USC in 1896, and in 1901 his Los Angeles College of Fine Arts was acquired by USC, where he was made the first dean of the USC College of Fine Arts, located on the Arroyo Seco in Garvanza (Highland Park), an artist's community. The Los Angeles School of Art and Design continued to operate after 1901 and does not appear to have been absorbed by USC.

The Los Angeles School of Art and Design had sketching parties to places like the San Gabriel Mission, Lincoln Park and the Mission Church in Los Angeles. Classes could have gone to Judson's studio or had him as a guest lecturer, or Winifred could have gone on her own time for further study. Still, there is no evidence that she graduated from USC.

Winifred shooting in a very stylish outfit. Girls learned to shoot just as early as the boys did.

Winifred worked as a draftsman for Title Insurance and Trust Co. for thirty-two years and also invested in real estate. She never married or had any children. After retirement in the 1940s, she moved back to the Bathey ranch full time and lived there for the rest of her life. An early photo album and drawings of Winifred's are owned by the Historical Society of the Crescenta Valley, and the pictures in this chapter are from her album. Other paintings of Winifred's are owned by the current owner of the Bathey

Winifred's drawing of the family home, done on April 30, 1900. *From the collection of the Historical Society of the Crescenta Valley.*

ranch. An exhibit of her work will soon be seen at the Lanterman Historical Museum Foundation in La Cañada Flintridge.

Winifred died on July 7, 1967, at the age of ninety-four at a convalescent hospital in Canoga Park. She is buried in the family plot at Odd Fellows Cemetery. The ranch was sold to the current owner. Imagine, only two owners in over 140 years!

Captain Bathey

Charles and Mary's oldest son, Herbert Theodore, was born in Boyle Heights on September 18, 1877. He worked as a farmer and builder, living in Los Angeles for forty years before moving back to the family home by 1948. He married Maude A. Starks about 1924, but no mention of her is found after a 1934 voter registration. Herbert served in the California National Guard for fifteen years, enlisting as a private. He was discharged as a captain in Company A, First Signal Corps, on January 4, 1918.

Herbert registered for the World War I draft on September 12, 1918:

> *Herbert Theodore Bathy, Born Sept. 13, 1877*
> *Nearest relative—Charles Theodore Bathey, 5632 Virginia Ave., Los Angeles, CA*
> *Medium height & build, grey eyes, light hair. Occupation—farmer in La Crescenta*

I find this registration a little strange because it is the only time he listed himself as a farmer. He had an office downtown, as listed on his voter registration, and there was no mention of his military service or honorable discharge. What is really odd is that his father was the person doing the registering.

Herbert held reunions of his Signal Corps at the Bathey ranch and was an avid deer hunter, featured in several newspaper articles about his adventures in Big Tujunga Canyon. He was a member of the Los Angeles Masonic Lodge and a lifelong Presbyterian. He granted several interviews to Grace Carpenter of the *Ledger* and provided valuable insight into his family and early valley history.

After retirement, he married Eudoxie Escalle Hall, daughter of early settler Pierre Escalle and widow of Vernon Hall, on September 23, 1949. In 1952, they moved to Santa Inez Valley, starting all over. They built a 1,700-pumice-block house by themselves, developed twenty-five acres of alfalfa, tended a vegetable garden and kept bees. They were featured in an extensive article in the December 22, 1957 *Los Angeles Times*:

> *Another interest shared by the Batheys is their bees. Both have worked with bees most of their lives and at one time Mrs. Bathey was one of the largest commercial bee operators in the La Crescenta area.*
>
> *Mrs. Bathey is now in the midst of completing a book called "I Found Life Among the Bees." Previously she has written "Crystal Christmas on the Desert." After completing the story of her life, she plans to embark on her third book. This will relate the experiences of the couple in pioneering on their ranch here and the building of their home together.*

Unfortunately, not one of these books has been located. Herbert died at the age of ninety-nine in Santa Inez on January 11, 1977. He outlived everyone in his family. He never had any children. He is buried with Eudoxie (d. February 1986) at Oak Hill Cemetery in Ballard, California.

Roy Alfred Bathey

Roy was the first child born in La Crescenta in June 1885. Family photos reflect an active life, with hiking and hunting and many beloved family pets. Roy and his sister Edith used to commute to La Crescenta Elementary School on their burros. Sadly, Roy died on February 9, 1903, at age seventeen of a burst appendix at Good Samaritan Hospital in Los Angeles. The official cause of death was peritonitis. One can only imagine the horrific trip to the hospital from the top of Briggs Avenue in a spring wagon over a bumpy, dirt road all the way to Los Angeles. Good Samaritan Hospital at that time was located at 924–34 West Seventh Street, almost seventeen miles from the Batheys' home. Roy is buried in the family plot at Odd Fellows Cemetery.

"Home Again" is the caption of Winifred's photo dated July 20, 1902. Winifred, Herbert and Allie were all working and living in Los Angeles. Note the rifles on the wall and the picture of Theodore Roosevelt.

Edith L. Bathey (Gibbs)

Edith was the youngest child, born on February 24, 1887, in La Crescenta. In 1904, after her mother's passing, she and her father moved to Hollywood near her other siblings. In 1920, she was a stenographer at Title Insurance & Trust Co., where her sister Winifred worked. About 1922, Edith married Harry Edwin Gibbs, a dentist. In the 1930 census, they were living in Tacoma, and she was a saleslady in a department store. They had no children, and they eventually moved back to La Crescenta, where Harry died in 1963. Edith stayed in La Crescenta but did not move back to the family ranch. She died on November 24, 1976, in La Crescenta and was interred at Odd Fellows Cemetery in the family plot with her husband.

Legacies

While the Batheys left no descendants, their presence in the valley is still here. The original ranch house and land remain intact at the intersection of Briggs Avenue and Shields Street. Herbert's interviews gave us personal insight into valley history, and Winifred's photos and paintings are still part of this world and will soon be on display at the Lanterman Museum.

2

Good Dr. Briggs and the Founding of La Crescenta

In the historical drama of La Crescenta, Benjamin Bennett Briggs is considered its hero, and research indicates that this was true. He founded, named and developed the town of La Crescenta. He helped, along with other residents, build the first elementary school and church, strove to bring electricity to the valley and donated land for the first store. While he was very charitable, we must not make him a saint. Many other settlers donated land, money and time for public projects, and Dr. Briggs, after all, was a businessman. It was in his best interest to encourage the growth of La Crescenta in order to sell off his subdivided property.

Young Benjamin B. Briggs. *Courtesy of Jacqueline Kennedy.*

Benjamin Bennett Briggs was born in Bristol, Ontario County, New York, on June 2, 1827, the seventh of ten children born to Thomas Briggs and Abigail Gregg. His brothers were Daniel Gregg, Silas, Abiel, George Gregg, John Gregg and Joseph Warren, and his sisters were Louisa Marie Crane,

Alinda Almeda Crane and Maria Antoinette Haskell. The family descended from Clement Briggs (1598–1648), who arrived in Plymouth from England in 1621 as a soldier. Ontario County was a good fruit-growing area, and the siblings would have grown up learning about horticulture, knowledge that later helped them become successful fruit growers. The family moved to Sharon, Medina County, Ohio, in 1835. Abigail Briggs died in 1837, and Thomas remarried twice.

Mexican-American War

In January 1847, when he was twenty years old, Benjamin and his brother George enlisted for six months in the army during the Mexican-American War, working as bridge builders/carpenters. They each earned forty-five dollars per month with one and a half rations. Benjamin enlisted in New Orleans and was discharged after three months. It is not known if he served in Texas or Mexico.

Gold Fever

On March 19, 1849, Benjamin and his brothers George and John set out from Sharon for the gold camps of California. Benjamin kept a journal of the trip with short notations of each day's activities and mileage. There are no extensive remarks, but it is a wonderful history. It was recently donated to the Doheny Library at the University of Southern California–Los Angeles. A typed transcript of the journal has been shared by a Briggs descendant. Benjamin seldom mentions any names, but they were traveling with other pioneers. They traveled first by water. After reaching St. Louis, Missouri, on April 13, they purchased an oxen team, which allowed them to travel an average of twenty miles a day.

Along the way, they would take a day or two to rest, and one time Briggs had mountain fever. On July 24, about 150 miles east of Morman City (Salt Lake City), Briggs noted, "Crossed a very level barron plane to a spring at the foot of the mountains I got accidently wounded." This is the only mention of a hunting accident; it left him with a bullet lodged in his spine. Supposedly, he stepped in front of a target at which one of his brothers was shooting. It has been stated that this held them up for eight weeks, but his diary contradicts that. He was weak and was bled. They stayed in camp five days. Then he was put in a wagon, and they traveled twelve miles. He was not able to ride, and they alternately rested and traveled. The accident slowed up their travel, but they did manage to keep going.

Over nine months after leaving Sharon, Ohio, they reached Yuba City on December 31, 1849. Benjamin decided that he was not strong enough to work the mines, but his brother George would not leave him, so they explored agricultural pursuits in the area. George became a pioneer fruit grower and was one of the first millionaires in California. One of his daughters, May, married Eugene Gould, and they built Gould Castle in La Crescenta. Brother John worked at the mines but soon also became a successful fruit grower, originating the Briggs peach. George and John stayed in California the rest of their lives; after about a year, Benjamin went back to Sharon.

Marriage and Family

Briggs married Abigale Crane, a schoolteacher in Putnam County, Indiana, on October 28, 1852. Abigale was born in Chatham, Massachusetts, on October 7, 1824, to Levi Lankon Crane and Sophia Dillingham Crane. Abigale and Benjamin had one daughter, Irene Crane Briggs, who was born on August 11, 1853, in Wadsworth, Ohio. Irene married Reverend Samuel Lawrence Ward on August 1, 1876, and immediately left for Persia, where they lived for twenty years. Due to Irene's poor health, they returned to the United States for long visits. They had six children and left many Briggs descendants.

In October 1859, while living in Sharon, Ohio, Briggs obtained a patent for an "Improved Apparatus for Laying Drain Tiles." Abigale had tuberculosis, and they moved to California, arriving in Marysville in November 1861 for a few months while waiting for their belongings to come around the horn. Brother George purchased Rancho Santa Paula in 1862. George took his family to Europe for a year to study vineyard production firsthand. Benjamin managed the Santa Paula property. Abigale died of tuberculosis on July 13, 1862. Briggs's sister, Maria A. Haskell, took Irene back east to live with relatives. Due to drought, the Santa Paula operation was not successful, and Benjamin went to work in the mines for three years. He eventually moved back to Sharon, Ohio, before 1865.

Medical School

Benjamin Briggs in Heidelberg, Germany, while attending medical school in 1865. Note the extra hand creeping on the arm of the chair. *Courtesy of Jacqueline Kennedy.*

Briggs decided he wanted to be a doctor, it is said, because he wanted to treat tubercular patients, but in fact, he had a reputation as a skilled surgeon. With daughter Irene, he left Hoboken for Germany in April 1865 aboard the *Teutonia*. The captain held up the voyage for four days to confirm the assassination of Abraham Lincoln on April 14, 1865. Briggs put Irene in boarding school and attended medical school in Heidelberg and Paris. After about a year, he returned to the United States and continued his studies here, attending a lecture series at Bellevue Hospital Medical School in New York. He attended the University of Michigan in 1868–69 and obtained additional medical/lecture degrees. He practiced as a surgeon in Crawfordsville, Indiana.

Mrs. Dr. Briggs

On May 25, 1870, Benjamin married his deceased wife's sister, Caroline Adelia Crane, the widow of Abiathar Crane. She was born on July 16, 1826, and had two children: Benjamin and Sophia (Ristine). In 1880, they were living in Crawfordsville, Indiana, and Benjamin was working as a doctor. Sadly, they had a daughter in Indiana who died before the age of three. As was the fashion then, she was referred to as Mrs. Dr. Briggs. Caroline was a founding member of the La Crescenta Presbyterian Church and the Shakespeare Club; she was sociable and hosted many guests at the Terrace.

In 1964, Anna Caroline Crane, granddaughter of Caroline, donated forty-seven letters, narratives and poems written by Mrs. Briggs to the Huntington Library Archives. Most of Caroline's letters were written to her daughter, Sophia Ristine, and son, Benjamin, when they were living back east and she was living in La Crescenta. They were mostly personal chitchat, but many important facts can be gleaned from them. She always referred to her husband as Dr. Briggs, spoke of his good nature and how hard he worked and mentioned how he always remained cheerful and uncomplaining even as his health declined. It appeared to have been a happy marriage.

She constantly mentioned the pure mountain air and the wonderful views from the Terrace. She wrote a narrative about the first Thanksgiving dinner at the La Crescenta Hotel, and it is reprinted here with the permission of the Huntington Library Archives:

> *Thanksgiving Day 1888*
> *The hotel in La Crescenta situated in the lovely mountain valley north of us, set its first Thanksgiving table Thursday.*
>
> *About fifty persons set down in it's well furnished dining room and feasted upon oyster soup, Turkey & Cranbery—, Chicken Pie & Olives, Roast Pork, Celery with Green Peas & Lynash, Potatoes, Radishes & Lettis Miner & Pumpkin Pie, Cake, Apples, Grapes & Oranges—all the substantials of an old fashioned New England dinner with the luxuries of our Semi-tropical sunshine. The whole house was filled with the perfume of Roses & Helitrope & other flowers with which it was lavishly adorned. The rooms have a delightfully comfortable—the parlors are cheerful & pleasant & the halls—& airy—Many of the guests rode up from Glendale in Greys hack, returning after dinner, others—the larger part; spent the night, to see the sunrise on the Mountains, & the fog lie over the city. The merry games of the evening when all gathered into the parlor with the sweet voices blending in song made it the fitting ending of an ideal Thanksgiving Day & when those who tired in the town said Goodnight & went out into the starlight—they felt that the place must seem a restful home like retreat to the lone invalid seeking health among strange faces in our pure mountain air.*

The Founding of La Crescenta

Like many early residents, Dr. Briggs moved to California to seek a better climate for his health. He first visited his brothers up north while deciding on a place to settle. With his sister, Maria A. Haskell, Dr. Briggs purchased 2,500 acres of multiple lots of land west of La Cañada from Jacob Lanterman and the estate of Adolphus W. Williams, as well as the property and water rights in Dunsmore and Cooks Canyon. He laid out a subdivision and sold it in ten-acre lots. His sister did not feel the land in La Crescenta was suitable for farming, so she sold her interests and moved with her children to La Cañada, where she purchased one hundred acres of land. She eventually sold out to Jesse Knight and moved the family back to San Francisco, where her husband and oldest son were living. In July 1882, Dr. Briggs was joined in a one-third partnership with his nephew, Asahel E. Briggs, son of his deceased brother, Abiel. It is stated that Asahel purchased his aunt Maria's property interests. Another nephew, Wallace, also was involved in some property transactions. Asahel and Wallace later attended medical school back east and became prominent doctors in Sacramento.

The first elementary school, built in La Crescenta in 1887 from cement that was shipped from Germany and donated by Dr. and Mrs. Briggs. It was located at Michigan (Foothill Boulevard) and Dyer Avenues. It was also the meeting place for the La Crescenta Presbyterian Church. *From Winifred Bathey's photo album.*

CRESCENTA CANYADA.

A HEALTHFUL AND BEAUTIFUL SPOT.

FINE CLIMATE. FINE SOIL.

PURE WATER AND PLENTY OF IT.

Only 11 miles North of Los Angeles.

CRESCENTA CANYADA

Is a Tract of 2,500 Acres of Land,

Situated near the base of the Sierra Madre Mountains, above the Verdugo Canon, known as FROSTLESS, WARM BRUSH LAND.

It is now being subdivided into Ten-Acre lots, each of which will have water right from a series of reservoirs now being made on the tract.

The Land will be Sold on Easy Terms,

With one-quarter cash down. A tract of Forty acres has been laid out as a Town site with a park and fountain. As a situation for invalids it is one of the finest in the world. Mount San Francisco Maria protects it from winds from the sea and the Sierra Madre from the north wind.

Special inducements will be given to parties who will put up a hotel, that would be filled all the year.

Inquire at the office of

T. E. ROWAN,

141 North Spring Street, Los Angeles.

Mr. A. E. Briggs will take pleasure in showing the land and giving all information about the same.

Send for descriptive circulars containing much valuable information concerning Southern California. Copies mailed free to any address. sep6w3m

An 1885 real estate ad promoting Briggs's 2,500-acre development offered in 10-acre lots in Crescenta Canyada, with one-quarter cash down. Nephew Asahel was the listing agent and in charge of showing the land and handling the transactions.

Dr. Briggs purchased, for his own residence, 160 acres of Section 22 from Theodor Pickens for $3,100. The deed was recorded in December 1882. The principal water rights in Pickens Canyon had been sold in 1878 to Ammoretta Lanterman, but there were two other water sources, and Briggs developed them. For their own domestic use, a well was dug. During his time in Germany, Dr. Briggs had learned of the use of cement in building, and he imported concrete from Germany to build his house. The concrete was used as ballast on the voyage over. His house is believed to have been the first concrete structure built in California. The home has been described as four large rooms, one of which was a bedroom. It had two chimneys and a wraparound porch. Briggs named the property "the Terrace," and this area was originally known as Crescenta Terrace and Avenue, later changed to the current Briggs Terrace and Briggs Avenue. The property is accessed by driving up Briggs Avenue and going right on Shields Avenue. The barn entrance was where the intersection of Shields Avenue and Freeman Avenue is now located. The residence was above and afforded wide views.

He helped found, along with other residents, the first elementary school and church in La Crescenta in 1887. The schoolhouse was built of cement and sheltered many local residents during the horrific windstorm of December 1887. In an isolated area, the importance of a schoolhouse cannot be overemphasized; it served many functions, including community meetings, church gatherings, social events and weddings.

The entire area was called La Cañada until Dr. Briggs named the valley Crescenta, which is a made-up word. Dr. Briggs thought that the view of the mountains resembled a crescent, and he Latinized that word to *Crescenta*. The area was referred to as Crescenta Canyada. The "La" was added in 1888 when a post office was established; the government did not want it to get confused with Crescent City, California. Even today, businesses and telephone directories still refer to the valley as Crescenta Canyada.

A Farmer's Life

A successful farmer diversifies his operations and does not rely on a single source of income, but Dr. Briggs's property was an agricultural showplace. He raised bees, had a vineyard that produced wine and raisins, harvested timber and grew oranges, lemons, figs, olives, walnuts, olives, apples, peaches, pears, plums, quinces, dates, bananas and pomegranates. An 1893 newspaper account states that the Briggs estate, at an altitude of 2,500 feet, grew Reisling, Muscatel, Zinfandel and Sultana grapes. To manage his orchards in a hilly location, he built a series of terraces.

He had a famous olive tree that warranted notice in the February 18, 1893 *Los Angeles Times*: "Dr. B.B. Briggs of Crescenta, Los Angeles county, has a tree that bore fifty gallons of fruit at thirteen years of age. Made into pickles, the crop would be worth, at wholesale, 75 cents per gallon, or $37.50."

Like most early settlers, Dr. Briggs raised bees, both for the cash crop and for pollinating his orchards. In a June 7, 1887 letter to his wife, Caroline, who was staying in Long Beach, he wrote about his honey crop:

> *I have been working with my bees, just finished the first extracting making a haul of about 300 lbs. and from this on for about 8 weeks. I must spend most of my time with them milking each hive about every 7 days and take from them their stores of the week. Many of them died during the long cold rain but those which came through are doing nicely now. So the next round I shall hope to get 600 or 700 lbs. but the extracting business though sweet is very hard work and could I hire some one to do it rightly I would be glad for I have so much else which ought to have my attention.*

The following Los Angeles newspaper article gives a wonderful description of the Terrace, as well as of life there. It is not dated, but since the property appears well established, the article is probably from sometime between 1890 and 1893. It is written in the rather flowery style of the time and has been edited:

> *The Terrace*
> *A Description of the Home of Mrs. Dr. Briggs*
> *Prof. R.C. French in writing from Los Angeles to the students of Massachusetts concerning the scenery and homes of California gives the following description of the home of Mrs. Dr. Briggs.*
>
> *Conspicuous among these homes, far up on the mountain side, on a plateau more than 2500 feet above the sea, is one known as "the Terrace."*
>
> *Should the riddle of this name be propounded to any among the uninitiated, it would be a dull mind indeed that could not solve it. Near the eastern edge of the valley is the first of a series of terraces which make up the ranch. These, extending far up the side of the mountain in diminishing sizes, suggest in their appearance the famous hanging gardens of Babylon. All the terraces are faced with walls of granite*

rock, which in many places are entirely concealed by flowering vines, hedges of roses, or bright colored geraniums. On this first terrace is a vineyard, not just bursting into life and verdure again. All deciduous vegetation in this semi-tropical climate, as in those that are colder, has its period of winter rest which warm days and frequent showers have no power to disturb. There is very little in a California vineyard to attract attention at any time of the year, for after the grapes are gathered, the vines are all cut back to the roots, so that in winter the vineyard is marked only by long lines of bare, brown stumps, while in summer the ground is covered by a matted mass of low trailing vines under whose broad leaves the grapes are sheltered from the blistering heat of the sun.

Climbing a little higher the next terrace is reached. Here is an orange orchard which, at this season is seen at its best, for it is now that the pure, unspotted white of the blossoms, the deep, glossy green of the leaves, and the bright gold of the ripe fruit, blend in such harmony of color that the orange tree stands without a peer for beauty among fruit trees. It is pleasant to linger here breathing the perfume laden air, and eating oranges without the necessity of thinking of each one as the fraction of a dozen, or feeling a little selfish because your luxury is not shared with some one else. Close at hand is a lemon orchard, the branches of whose trees now, as at all times in the year, are thick with bloom, and bend low with growing and ripe fruit. Next above is a terrace which is bordered by a thick Monterey cypress hedge and on which fig and orange trees alternate with quince and pomegranate.

On the terraces higher up the mountain are large orchards of deciduous fruit trees, such as peach, pear, plum and apples, while yet higher are more vineyards and orange orchards. On this extensive ranch is raised every kind of fruit grown in southern [climes] *except pineapples. But to get a good idea of what is produced here the fruit house must be visited. On one side are long lines of casks of wine, the vintage of many seasons. Crates of oranges and lemons are packed ready for marked. Figs, in five and ten pound boxes are ----- or ----- with larger boxes of raisins. Here also are barrels of pickled olives. Sacks of almonds and English walnuts are piled on the floor. It is probable that very few ranches in southern California are so fortunate in the varied character of their soil or have such difference in elevation as to admit of such a variety of products. There is very little land in California that is valuable for agricultural purposes if there are no facilities for its irrigation. Ample provision is made for this on the Terrace ranch and a constant and sure supply of water occurred. Above the highest terrace is a large reservoir, which is kept constantly full of the purest water from springs far up on the mountain. From this reservoir water is conducted to the different terraces by a system of pipes. The water for domestic use, however, comes directly from the spring itself.*

From the valley a broad carriage drive bordered by olive trees winds round the terraces, past the lodge where the employees live, and the corral in which the cattle and horses are kept, till it at last emerges upon the terrace where several years ago the present owner, a retired physician, built his home—a house as much the product of the climate as anything about it, and as unsuited to New England as the palms and banana trees by which it is surrounded. It is so situated that not a breeze that blows or a ray of sunshine that lights upon it, can fail to find access to its most secluded corner. Extending entirely about the house is a broad, shaded veranda upon which every room opens from two doors. Here the social life of the family is carried on, here the gifted hostess receives her guests, and here in the evenings of nearly everyday the family gathers for the reading of the daily papers, the latest magazine of the favorite authors.

Many an evening has the mother of this home made memorable as she unfolded to her delighted listeners the mysteries of Browning or made merry over the lighter verse of James Whitcomb Riley. From the veranda a spacious lawn slopes to an orange grove. One looks here in vain for the beautiful maple or the graceful elm so common about New England homes, and can but feel that among the trees he misses familiar friends, though their places are filled by others of more majestic size and elegant proportions. Shading a fountain in whose cool depths multitudes of gold fish dart back and forth like sunbeams at a game of hide and seek, stands a broad-spreading pepper tree which, when seen in the distance looks very much like

An 1885 picture of the Terrace. Family members on the porch are, *from left*: Caroline C. Briggs, S. Paul Ward, Benjamin B. Ward, Irene Briggs Ward, Asahel Briggs and Dr. B. Briggs. The grapevines were brought from Persia by son-in-law S. Lawrence Ward. The home offered magnificent views—on a clear day, all the way to Pasadena. *Courtesy of Carlton Ward Kennedy.*

the common weeping willow. Beyond is a magnolia tree, and farther down the slope at irregular intervals grow the acacia, the bay, the camphor, and the rubber tree, while clumps of roses, dates, palms and bananas, occupy convenient corners.

Sanitarium

Dr. Briggs intended to open a sanitarium on his property, and at times the Terrace has been called the Briggs Sanitarium. According to newspaper accounts, while it appears that people occasionally stayed at the Terrace for extended periods of time to rest, no actual sanitarium was established. Caroline Briggs mentions in her letters that Dr. Briggs still hoped to open a sanitarium, but he was too weak to do so. With four rooms and only one bedroom, there was not a lot of room in the house for many patients or visitors.

Timber Harvesting

Like many settlers, Dr. Briggs harvested timber in the steep hills around his property. In the popular view of valley history, timber harvesting has been perceived as being somehow evil or nefarious, which is not the case. Since the days of the early missions, San Gabriel Mountain timber has been cut down, sometimes for crude buildings but in later days for fuel for the growing metropolis of Los Angeles. While there probably was illegal timber harvesting in the San Gabriels, this would have been done before land was settled and occupied. Timber had to be brought down the mountain, and permission would have been required to haul it across occupied land. The harvesting done by Dr. Briggs was under a legally acquired timber harvesting permit approved on April 5, 1886, for eighty acres in Section 22.

A copy of Briggs's land patent sale of timberland application dated April 13, 1885, has been obtained from the National Archives in Washington, D.C. His witnesses for the application were Jacob L. Lanterman and Frank D. Lanterman; they attested to the fact that the land was only suitable for timber harvesting. Dr. Briggs paid $2.50 for the acreage.

Chinamen and the Mountain Lion

Dr. Briggs employed Chinese laborers to work on his extensive orchards. They had a separate bunkhouse on the property, which was a step up from some of the shanties and tents in which many were forced to live. Their lives were hard and lonely, with virtually no chance of ever having wives or children. The Chinese who came to work in California were mainly from the Canton region of southeast China, near the port city of Guangzhou. They spoke a Cantonese dialect, not Mandarin. The Chinese operated under the clan system with a foreman who would have spoken some English. With the completion of the transcontinental railroad in 1869, the Chinese workers found themselves unemployed. They migrated to other areas and established "Chinatowns." When they arrived in Los Angeles, they would immediately go to one of the Tong societies, where they would be put on the work rolls. Brother Silas Briggs lived in Sharon, Ohio, but visited the Terrace for extended periods and helped with operations. The following article is from the *Los Angeles Herald* of August 24, 1884:

> *A Battle with a Lion*
> *The Monster Slain Within Sight of the City—Chinamen Feast Upon Lion Meat, All the Same as Chicken.*
>
> *It will be a matter of great surprise to many of the readers of the* Herald *to know that a powerful lion was this week killed on Crescenta Cañada, in full view of the City of Los Angeles. Since the lion is dead the settlers think "a living dog is better than a dead lion," and all brag about having had a part and lot in the killing of the King of Beast.*
>
> *The facts about the demise of the great lion of La Cañada appear to be these: Mr. Silas Briggs, brother of the proprietors' of Crescenta Cañada, and a Nimrod of the royal line, on Tuesday took a walk near the residence of Dr. B.B. Briggs in search of game, and when the Doctor heard the crack of his brother's rifle he hurried up the heights to help bring in a deer or mountain sheep for his fine sanitarium, and took the Chinese cook along to help bring in the toothsome venison or sturdy steaks of bear, knowing that "brother Si" never wastes powder and ball. Before they had proceeded far they heard the agonizing roar of a wounded lion that was struggling and writhing in pain and showing two rows of ivory that had no need for a dentist. None of the party were anxious to investigate the matter at short range till the quadruped lost his vitality, when he was taken down to the house where all the Chinamen at work in the neighborhood congregated and*

discussed the lion question. When the skin of the monarch was removed the Chinamen were enthusiastic in praise of the delicious and shiny meat. "Heap good!" "Me like him all same chicken." "Belly good."

The Mongolians manifested such an affection for meat "alle same chicken," that the carcass weighing two hundred pounds was "given to the heathen for an inheritance," and they made a great feast of lion soup, roast lion, lion fricassee, lion à la mode, lion stew, and boiled lion and rice, till their chopsticks wore out with exercise.

The whole camp lionized three days on the savory meat, while the white man got only the skin of the beast for his risk and trouble.

While some of us may tire of our present-day political correctness, the tone of this article is cringe-worthy and a good example of the cultural mindset of the nineteenth century. There is still the occasional mountain lion sighting in the valley.

DEATH COMES TO DR. BRIGGS

It was thought that Benjamin B. Briggs died as a result of an operation to remove the bullet lodged in his spine, but in one of Mrs. Briggs's letters, it is revealed that her husband had the operation in 1887 and survived. He actually died of tuberculosis on February 15, 1893. The following is from a Los Angeles newspaper dated February 28, 1893:

La Crescenta
Death of Dr. Briggs, the Founder of this Colony
La Crescenta, Feb. 28—A shadow of sorrow is cast over our whole community by the death of Dr. B.B. Briggs, on the 15th of this month. Though he had been ill with consumption for some time, when the final summons came, no one but himself seemed prepared for his death; but he had indeed "got his house in order" for all time, having put all his business in California into the hands of his nephew, Mr. George Crane of Ventura, with absolute power to act, and every[thing] *was arranged to save complication and trouble. He met death with a calmness which no one else could summon.*

He will be greatly missed from our midst, as he has long been the mainspring of the entire colony, coming here before any of the present residents, with one or two exceptions, and together with Messrs. Childress and Lowell of Los Angeles, buying most of this valley, which was named "Crescenta" by Dr. Briggs, from the crescent shape of the mountains back of it; they subdivided it into 10-acre lots, developed water and laid out the townsite. Dr. Briggs afterward bought out his partners, made other large purchases and conducted the enterprise alone.

He has always subscribed largely to all public enterprises, giving 10 acres of land to the church organization, besides generously contributing money when-ever asked; he gave two and a half acres on the townsite for a park, set out trees, built the fountain basin, etc., gave two town lots for a store, general lots for a hotel, besides many more gifts for the good of the place. He had recently finished a fine large reservoir for storing the water for the town site. He had looked forward to the good of the place in the future, and disliking to be thanked, yet his monument is in the hearts of those to whom he has been kind and helpful, and will endure forever.

His funeral, at his home, The Terrace, was attended by nearly all the residents of the place, and his body, at his express wish, was taken to Los Angeles and cremated at the Rosedale cemetery. Dr. Briggs was well known in Los Angeles, as well as in this locality, having done business there for many years. He left a wife and one daughter, (who is now in Persia), besides a step-son and daughter, the latter of whom was with him at the time of his death.

Dr. Briggs was cremated at Rosedale Cemetery in Los Angeles. The cemetery records indicate that no one picked up his ashes, and they were buried in an unknown location at the cemetery. In an unusual set of circumstances, there is a large pyramid monument for Dr. Briggs and his first wife, Abby Crane, at Sharon Center Cemetery in Ohio. He most likely purchased the monument after his first wife died. It had previously been believed that he was buried somewhere on the Terrace property.

Although Dr. Briggs is not buried there, there is a memorial pyramid for him and his first wife, Abby, at Sharon Cemetery, Ohio. *Courtesy of the Medina County Cemetery Preservation Society.*

After her husband's death, Caroline Briggs moved back to Crawfordsville to live with her daughter. Dr. Briggs's probate file cannot be located at the Hall of Records or in the Huntington Archives, but Caroline probably received a life interest in the Terrace. The property was managed by early French immigrant Pierre Escalle, a stonemason and farmer who maintained the extensive orchards that would have provided an income for Caroline. Briggs's daughter, Irene Ward, and her family would occasionally stay at the Terrace during the time Reverend Ward was a minister in Glendale. After Caroline died in 1916, the property was sold and eventually torn down in 1965. A new residence was built near the intersection of Shields Street and Freeman Avenue.

Benjamin Bennett Briggs leaves his name in Briggs Avenue and Briggs Terrace and has been remembered for his vision of La Crescenta with a large plaque on the floor of the atrium at the new La Crescenta Library dedicated in January 2010.

3

Delia W. Dunks, Health Resort Operator

Unless they are quite famous or left behind journals, nineteenth-century women are difficult to write about. They do not leave as much of a trail as do men. They did not vote or serve in the military, and many times they did not own property. In newspapers and obituaries, their first names were seldom given. Delia Woodbury Dunks lived in Lansing, Michigan, for many years and later knew many of the original Crescenta Valley settlers, including Colonel Adolphus Williams and Jacob Lanterman. When these men originally came to California looking for a suitable place to settle, they stayed at Delia's boardinghouse in La Cañada.

Delia A. Woodbury was born on February 14, 1829, in Mendon, New York. Her parents were Ulysses Woodbury and Lucy Durand. She had had five younger siblings: Mark, Carrie, Helen, John and Daniel. Before 1839, the family moved to Lansing, Michigan, where they were farmers. About 1850, she married Harris H. Dunks, who was born in 1815 in New York. They resided in Lansing and were farmers in the 1860 census. They cannot be found in the 1870 census, but records indicate that they were living in Los Angeles by then.

Like many early Crescenta Valley residents, the Dunkses came west due to health problems, in this case Harris's poor health. Delia and Harris were among the earliest settlers of the Crescenta Valley. According to a descendant of one of Delia's sister Helen's stepchildren, they came to Los Angeles sailing around Cape Horn, bringing a lot of furniture with them. While the transcontinental railroad was completed in 1869, it only went to

Delia's rocker, which was brought from Michigan and shipped around the Horn in the 1860s. Think of all the early settlers who sat in this chair. *Courtesy of James McHargue.*

San Francisco and did not connect to Los Angeles until 1876. Some of the Dunkses' furniture and possessions have been passed down to Helen's descendants.

Delia's obituary states that the Dunkses came to Los Angeles in 1869. They most likely lived and worked in Los Angeles for a while and started developing their La Cañada land part time while still working in the city. Harris Dunks is listed in the 1872 voter registration as a resident of Los Angeles. According to Delia's witness statement on her land patent application dated October 2, 1878, they settled on the 160-acre northwest corner of Section 36 in November 1873. This was likely when they settled permanently in La Cañada, but they had probably been in the area earlier. By 1878, they had built a house and barn and had planted a twenty-five-acre orchard. They had also secured the water rights in Dunks Canyon.

Harris died on January 22, 1878, in La Cañada. No death record or burial information has been found for him; as was the custom in the early days, he was probably buried on the property. There are accounts that at least three people were buried there. The value of the estate was estimated at $3,300, consisting of real estate, one horse, one mare, a cow, a wagon, household goods and farming tools. As Delia and Harris did not have any children, Delia inherited the estate and became the head of household for legal purposes.

Two months after Harris's death, Delia was one of the witnesses in the March 1878 *Lanterman v. Williams* appeals trial. The trial was a property dispute; the transcript runs 176 pages and includes witness testimony from several early residents. If Harris Dunks had been alive, he would have been the one to testify. Delia's testimony runs 10 pages, and the excerpt that follows is from *Sources of History*:

> *I reside north of the Cañada, on section 36. Have lived there 7 years. Have known Colonel Williams for over 20 years. Williams came to my house, north of the Canada, Sept. 33d, 1875. Lanterman came December 4th, 1875. They boarded with me, some time. Our land adjoins the ranch on the north. In plain sight of it. Have often heard conversation between Lanterman and Williams in regard to this grant. Have seen a map of the grant. It was gotten up in my house. The Doctor did not have much to say about it. I suppose their interests were equal from all the conversations I heard, both as to land and water. About two weeks after they purchased the grant I heard a memorandum of an agreement read in the front room of my house. Mr. Dunks, myself, the Doctor; the Colonel and his son, Charles. The agreement was read by Charles Williams. After it was read my husband said, "I think that is all O.K; I don't see that there can be any trouble about it." The Colonel then said that he had given the Doctor the right to make the first choice of lots. The Doctor made no remarks that I am aware of now. He acquiesced I suppose. The division was made according to a map that was made at our place by Col. Williams. I suppose that map was present then. As it was screwed upon the table it might have been there for a month. There was also a map pinned on the wall. The first one that was made was pinned on the wall, and there was a better one made; I suppose a more correct one. The map represented the out boundaries, avenues and lots of the rancho, numbered from one to over forty. I think Lanterman had the odd numbered lots and Williams the even ones. After that they commenced building houses on their lots respectively, while they were at my house boarding. After their map was made and the agreement was read. I suppose they were running lines as they took the instrument from my house. I suppose Col. Williams and his son used the instruments. The Doctor made no objection that I heard to the line being pointed out by Williams. Nor to the map on the table. The agreement was based upon this map. My husband rented five acres of land from Lanterman. I suppose it was according to this map. We calculated that piece of ground came on his. He had to pay rent to Dr. Lanterman if he occupied it. No protests to that was made by Williams, he was perfectly willing he should occupied it.*

VERDUGO HEIGHTS

Delia operated Verdugo Heights, which at different times has been referred to as a sanitarium, health resort, hotel and boardinghouse. It was not a sanatorium, which is more of a hospital setting that provides medical care and treatment for long-term illnesses such as tuberculosis. An undated newspaper advertisement for Verdugo Heights reads:

MOUNTAIN RETREAT
Verdugo Heights
This sanitarium, thirteen miles from Los Angeles, is situated at an altitude of 1800 feet on the south slope of the Sierra Madre mountains. The situation is peculiarly dry and healthful, free from fogs, and is an excellent home for those affiliated with pulmonary difficulties. Table well supplied. Pure mountain spring water. Terms moderate, $8 per week.

References: Burch and Boal, Mr. J.W. Stowbridge, St. Charles Hotel, Mr. E.B. Milar.

Free Conveyance leaves Burch and Boal's, corner of Spring and First streets, every Wednesday and Saturday at 1:30 P.M.

Mrs. D.W. DUNKS, Prop'r.

Verdugo Heights was well known and was visited in 1882 by author Helen Hunt Jackson on her trip around California doing research for her book *Ramona*. In her diary from that trip, there is an entry stating that she visited Mrs. Dunks at Verdugo Heights:

January, Sunday 15, 1882
Went with Mr. Kinney to Verdugo Heights—Mrs. Dunks—walked down to Brooks—Splendid day—clouds & mists with breaks—& sun in distance on the Pacific ocean.

Delia and Theodor Pickens entered into a partnership after her husband died in 1878. A story has been passed down about their partnership and is recounted in *Sources of History*:

OLD FEUD
We remember the stories about Theodore Pickens and his partner Mrs. D.W. Dunks. They operated a sanitarium on what is now the Frank P. Doherty place and for some years they got along most amicably with each other. But both

were stubborn and most determined. When an argument arose over credit to a houseguest, open warfare broke out. They decided to divide their property—Pickens agreed to move one half of the sanitarium building to his own property to the south. In the meantime, they decided to divide the milk from their Jersey cow. Pickens to milk two teats each day and Mrs. Dunks had the other two. One weekend Pickens took a hunting trip was gone for two days. The story goes that Mrs. Dunks would not milk the Pickens side of the cow; the poor animal almost died from milk-bag-congestion. When Pickens returned Mrs. Dunks directed him to leave immediately, to move his ½ of the sanitarium building and to remove himself and his belongings.

This story is rather hard to believe. How long it takes a cow to get mastitis, I do not know, but not milking it would have been an extremely cruel thing for Delia to do to an innocent animal, not to mention one in which she had financial interest.

The partnership most likely ended before December 20, 1882, when, according to the *Los Angeles Times*, "Theodor Pickens sold to Delia W. Dunks, an undivided ½ interest in Verdugo Heights including improvements in Section 36 for $1000."

The portion Pickens is reported to have moved was relocated to 1117 Green Lane. It is unlikely that they sawed the main house in half; the portion that Pickens took was either a separate structure on the property or a later addition that was easily separated from the original building. A new home was built on the site in 1996, and the county assessor's office shows no record of an older structure being on the property.

Mrs. Dunks's portion of the original house was at what later was given the address of 1029 Vista Del Valle. There exist several pictures of Verdugo Heights at various times, and the structure greatly varies. One photo shows a main house with several additions of various styles.

There is no record that Pickens ever lived at Verdugo Heights. In the 1880 census, he is listed as a separate head of household, and Delia is noted with four boarders (including a housekeeper) residing at Verdugo Heights. Delia's and Pickens's names are not listed next to each other in the census. Delia was thirteen years older than Pickens, and what their exact relationship was is not known.

Delia sold some parcels of land and half the water rights in Dunks Canyon. According to the *Los Angeles Times* of December 3, 1892, "Real estate transfers Delia W. Dunks to Ernest J. Kussell, land in E1/4 section 36, T 2 N, R 13 W, $3000."

Pickens working at Verdugo Heights when he was in partnership with Delia Dunks, early 1880s.

No record has been found to determine exactly when Delia sold the rest of her property, but by 1899 she was living in East Los Angeles at 340½ Day Street with her sister Helen (Nellie), Helen's daughter Alice and other family members. She may have had income from leasing her land and income from the water in Dunks Canyon. Delia died of heart failure in Los Angeles on November 18, 1908, and there was a short notice of her death in the *Los Angeles Times* on November 20, 1908:

> *Obituary of Delia W. Dunks, sister of Helen R. Caldwell*
> *Dunks, Mrs. Delia W. Dunks, born February 14, 1829, at Mendon, New York, died in Los Angeles, November 18, 1908. Mrs. Dunks came to California in 1869 residing many years in La Canyada Valley, and recently with her sister Mrs. Helen W. Caldwell.*

Delia is buried in Evergreen Cemetery in East Los Angeles in the Caldwell family plot; her grave is located to the right of the Caldwell monument next to that of her niece Alice.

What do we know about Delia? Well, we certainly know she could milk a cow! She was born and raised on a farm and knew all about that life. Was she sweet, shy and retiring? Hardly. She was hardworking and operated Verdugo Heights for over twenty years. A successful innkeeper has to be welcoming, hospitable, accommodating and a good cook. She was the first independent businesswoman in the valley.

What Happened to Verdugo Heights?

After Delia finally sold all her property, it was transferred to several owners and was used as a private residence. In the 1900 census, there was no one in La Cañada listed as operating a sanitarium or boardinghouse. The house was extensively remodeled; only one portion of a wall was kept, and in the end it bore no resemblance to the original structure. It was located east of Angeles Crest Highway, north of Vista Del Valle between Haskell Street and La Cañada Boulevard.

One well-known owner was Edwin W. Sargent (and his wife, Alma). Edwin was a title attorney and founded the Los Angeles Abstract Company in 1887. This company became Title Insurance and Trust in 1895. He was called "Judge Sargent" by people in the valley, but in actuality he was not a judge. He died in 1929, and his wife lived at the property for a few more years.

Frank P. and Sarah Doherty lived down the street from the Sargents and, by 1938, had purchased and moved into the former Verdugo Heights. They lived there for many years raising their family of six children and were very involved with community, church and political organizations. In November 1952, Verdugo Heights was included on the St. Bede's Catholic Church open house fundraiser. In January 1953, Mrs. Doherty hosted the first meeting of the Jose Verdugo Chapter of the Daughters of the American Revolution at the home. The house was referred to as "palatial" and had a long driveway

The much-remodeled Verdugo Heights before it was torn down in the 1960s. *Courtesy of the Lanterman Museum Historical Foundation.*

lined with cypress trees. The property was assigned the address of 1029 Vista Del Valle.

The Dohertys lived there until about 1964; they were living at another address in La Cañada in 1965. The home was torn down, and a new housing development was built on the street in 1966. Glenola Park (formerly Triangle Park) at Angeles Crest Highway and Vista Del Valle was part of Delia's northwest Section 36.

A Dubious Legacy

A longtime source of irritation for La Cañada residents living in the Vista Del Valle and El Vago areas is the wild band of peafowl that roam the area, destroying plant life, fowling the ground and annoying everyone with their loud shrieking. They are relatives of the pheasant. Male peafowl are called peacocks, females are peahens and the youngsters are peachicks. They roam in bands of ten to ninety and generally live about fifteen years in the wild.

Peafowl historically were considered the privilege of royalty and nobility; they were a status symbol and were highly prized in the Victorian era. They

A blue Indian peacock and peahen of the type that still roams La Cañada, much to the chagrin of some residents. *Courtesy Stockvault.net.*

were originally imported from India to Southern California about 1875 by Elias J. (Lucky) Baldwin for his Arcadia ranch. It is estimated he had a band of about fifty there.

Peacocks were good for meat and egg production; being omnivorous, they kept the snails, rattlesnakes and small rodents at bay. They were also good watchdogs and would give their loud and piercing calls when someone or something came around. Breeding peacocks and raising them for egg production was a popular hobby among women in the nineteenth century.

According to Don Mazen in his book *The History of La Cañada Flintridge*, when Edwin W. Sargent purchased ninety acres of Delia's Section 36 property, the peafowl were already there. Since the area was not populated, they were no problem. When Frank Doherty purchased the property from Sargent, he welcomed the peafowl, as they helped control the rattlesnake population. When Doherty sold the property in 1964, he tried to round up the peafowl and donate them to the Los Angeles County Arboretum, but he did not catch all of them, and it is their descendants that roam the area today.

While we cannot say for sure that Delia is the person who brought the peafowl to the valley, all the facts point to her as the likely culprit.

4

James Franklin Dunsmoor, aka Frank Dunsmore

In our daily lives in the Crescenta Valley, we come across many references to Dunsmore: Canyon, Avenue, Park, Debris Basin and Elementary School, as well as Dunsmuir Sediment Debris Basin. After whom were these places named? Actually, due to early incorrect record keeping, the name was misspelled. The correct name was actually Dunsmoor. While the Dunsmoor family lived in the valley for only a few years, they have left their mark, and their story deserves telling. Frank's and his wife Hattie's lives offer a rich history of nineteenth-century America, and they represent the character of the people who settled here.

James Franklin Dunsmoor was born on March 19, 1838, at Temple, Franklin County, Maine. By the early 1850s, the family had moved and was farming land that was called the Old Military Reserve, now Fort Snelling, in St. Paul, Minnesota. His parents were James Adam and Almira Mosher Dunsmoor. They had six sons who lived to adulthood, and all were very successful.

Frank, as he was known, was working on his father's farm when the Civil War began in April 1861. Thinking the war would be short, Lincoln called for seventy-five thousand volunteers for three months' service. Frank was twenty-three when, on May 23, 1861, he was mustered into Company D, First Minnesota Volunteer Infantry, Lincoln Guards, at Fort Snelling. The enrolling clerk misspelled his name as Dunsmore, but this was later corrected in military records. The unit was issued temporary uniforms consisting of red wool shirts, black or dark blue pants, black felt hats and two pairs of socks each, along with blankets and mess kits. The young men had been acquainted with firearms since they were old enough to hold them, and many had experience serving with the local militias organized for protection against local Indians.

On June 22, 1861, the men left Fort Snelling, traveling on riverboats and various railroad transports. They arrived in Washington, D.C., on June 26. They were given an enthusiastic send-off parade in Minneapolis and were greeted along the way by supportive crowds. They camped near the Capitol Building, spending their time constantly drilling, and participated in the first major battle of the Civil War.

The Northern newspapers had pressured the government for a decisive victory: take Richmond and end the war. The three-month enlistments were expiring, and the Union unfortunately entered into a premature battle using inexperienced and unprepared troops. The First Battle of Bull Run—or the First Battle of Manassas, as it is known in the South—was the first major battle of the Civil War, and it was a Union rout. After this battle, both sides knew that the conflict was going to be much bloodier and longer than they had anticipated. It was reported that spectators from Washington, D.C., drove in their carriages to watch the battle.

Lincoln immediately signed a bill calling for an enlistment of 500,000 and three years of service. It was not until after Bull Run that the First Minnesota got proper uniforms. The following excerpt is from the First Minnesota unit history:

> *July 21, 1861—Battle of Bull Run*
> *The First fell in at 2:00 a.m. and started marching four hours later. The regiment was ordered to support Rickett's Battery in an attack on Henry House Hill. Cos. "A" & "F" led the attack, and were separated from the regiment to the right of the battery by the confusion in deploying the guns. Colonel Gorman ordered the men to hold fire on the attacking 33rd Virginia because he thought they were Yankees. Ricketts battery was lost and recaptured several times before finally falling to the rebels. In between the rebel attacks the regiment received grape and canister from a masked battery. Javan Irvine, a civilian attached to Co. A, captured the Lt. Col. of the 2nd Mississippi, the highest ranking Confederate taken that day. Sgt. John Merritt of Co. "K" was awarded the Medal of Honor for taking brief possession of a rebel flag. After discovering that they were isolated, Lt. Col. Miller ordered the two companies to retreat. The regiment then covered the western flank of the Union retreat.*
>
> *The First Minnesota was one of the last regiments to leave the battlefield, and suffered the highest casualties of any northern regiment: 48 killed,*

83 wounded, 23 wounded and missing, and 30 missing (the number of missing taken prisoner is uncertain—most returned to the unit).

At the battle, Frank was disabled and taken off the field. On August 1, 1861, he was discharged for disability due to paralysis of the eye. The maximum at that time for a disability pension was eight dollars per month, with the amount determined by the severity of the injury. In 1873, Frank filed for a disability pension and received four dollars per month. He was a member of the First Minnesota veterans' organization all his life.

Frank returned to Minnesota and moved to the Litchfield area in Meeker County, where he took a homestead about a mile from the Litchfield stockade. Due to potential Indian trouble, he took up lodging in a house located inside the stockade that the settlers had erected in Litchfield. He joined a local militia formed as a self-defense force to protect the citizens of Minnesota during the 1862 Sioux uprising. He served with his future father-in-law, John C. Hoffman, for two months.

In the spring of 1863, he moved into the house of John C. and Mary Hoffman as a boarder and probably as protection for the family. John, unfortunately, was killed by Indians in September. Frank fell in love with their daughter, and he and Harriet "Hattie" Murdock Hoffman were married on December 20, 1863. They took a wedding trip to Minneapolis and established their own homestead in Todd County, which they farmed for eleven years. It was here that many of their twelve children were born.

Moving to California

In 1873, Frank's mother and father and brothers Charles and John moved to Los Angeles, and Frank and Hattie soon followed, traveling nine days on a train from Minneapolis to San Francisco, two days and nights on a steamer to Wilmington and then by train to Los Angeles. They spent a year in El Monte and then moved to Los Flores Canyon (Dunsmore) on railroad land, where Frank was a commercial beekeeper. In the 1880 census, the family was listed as Frank Dunsmore, apiarist, Clara (incorrect), Charlie, Jimmi, Myra, Minnie, Roxanna and twenty-four-year-old Chinese laborer Foo Ching. One of their daughters, Pinky, died at age six while they were living in the valley.

Frank's land in Dunsmore Canyon was located in what is now Deukmejian Wilderness Park. The land was railroad land, which he sold to Benjamin B. Briggs

Dunsmore and Markridge Road. Below Markridge was the rancho and above was public land, now Deukmejian Wilderness Park. *Courtesy of the author.*

on June 26, 1883. Briggs did not develop the land but purchased it for investment and for the water flowing out of Dunsmore and the adjacent Cook Canyon. In 1886, Briggs sold the property to George Le Mesnager, who developed the property as a vineyard. It is now part of Deukmejian Wilderness Park.

Like many early valley families, the Dunsmores moved away so their children could go to school and probably to be less isolated. They settled in Tropico, an early settlement that is now part of Glendale. In the 1884 voter registration, Frank was listed as a schoolteacher. He also was a school commissioner and helped establish the Glendale school system.

In 1892, after the double wedding of two of their daughters in Glendale, Frank and Hattie moved to a "timber claim" in Antelope Valley, near where their son Charles and his family lived. They cleared thirty acres of timberland and planted wheat. They dug a well 140 feet deep to get water.

About 1898, they moved to Lancaster, and at the time of the 1900 census, Frank was sixty-two and Hattie was fifty-three. They resided with two children, Emma and William, as well as Frank's eighty-two-year-old mother, Almira. There they served as the postmaster and postal clerk for fifteen years. The post office in Lancaster was in a room in their home located on the south side of Tenth Street, just east of Beach Avenue. Old-timers used to say that this was the center of life in Lancaster about 6:00 p.m., when the mail arrived. After fifteen years with the post office, the Dunsmores retired and moved to Santa Monica.

Frank died in Santa Monica on November 19, 1915, at the age of seventy-seven. He is buried at the Evergreen Cemetery in East Los Angeles. When he died, there were several obituaries for him in various publications. He was very well thought of and respected. Even though he had been gone from Glendale for more than twenty years, he was remembered in a gracious obituary in the *Glendale Evening News* on Tuesday, November 30, 1915:

> *Death of Pioneer—Valley Pioneer Dies*
> *After an illness of some months, Mr. J.F. Dunsmoor, died at Santa Monica Nov. 20. Mr. Dunsmoor was 77 years of age, a Civil War veteran and an all-round good citizen. Before Glendale and Tropico had been christened, along in the early '00s, the Dunsmoor family lived on the San Fernando road near the Gal winery. Mr. Dunsmoor was one of the first school trustees in this section, acting in that capacity when there was only one schoolhouse in this part of the valley and continuing as such until there were three school districts in the immediate neighborhood of his home.*
>
> *Mr. Dunsmoor was an active Republican in politics in those early days but was always to be found lined up with that portion of the party which objected to the influence of the Southern Pacific company in the political affairs of the state. He was brother to Chas. F. Dunsmoor, at one time county clerk and later bank commissioner; of Dr. John M. Dunsmoor of Los Angeles, and of A.V. Dunsmoor, who until a year ago for a long time owned the circulation route of the* Los Angeles Times *in this section.*
>
> *Mr. Dunsmoor went from Glendale to Antelope valley where he was appointed postmaster at Lancaster, serving in that capacity for about 15 years. He was a quiet, unassuming public-spirited citizen, upright in character and of the kind that leave the world poorer for their leaving it.*

Hattie (Harriet) Murdock Hoffman Dunsmoor

Hattie, as she was always known, had an equally interesting background and life as her husband. She was born in Pittsburgh on August 22, 1846, to John Conrad Hoffman and Mary Dupew. They were farmers and moved to Indiana and then to Todd County, Minnesota, when Hattie was very young.

John C. Hoffman served in the Civil War for two months as a first lieutenant. Hattie had five brothers: John, Cornelius, Thomas, Andrew and Oliver. Her brother John, also a Civil War veteran, ended up settling in Lancaster.

Hattie's father was killed by Indians in September 1863 in the aftermath of the Sioux Wars of 1862. Frank Dunsmoor was boarding at the house at the time.

Hattie and Frank had twelve children, eight of whom lived to adulthood: Lemuel L., Charles Irving, James C., Mary Almira (Myra), Minnie Belle, Emma (Birdie), Roxanna, Cynthia, Adelaide (Pinky), Frederick Albert and William Adelbert. Her last child was William, born in 1891, when she was forty-five years old with most of her children grown.

Hattie wrote a narrative of her life in 1925 entitled "One of the Girls of '61," an invaluable look at nineteenth-century life. She included the following comments about their life in California:

> *In 1874 we came to California in an Emigrant car attached to a freight train. We were 9 days coming from Minneapolis to San Francisco. We reached San Francisco on Christmas Day. Then we were two days and two nights on the water coming down from San Francisco to Wilmington. We went from Wilmington to Los Angeles on the only railroad then in Southern California.*
>
> *My husband's mother and father lived on Grand Avenue at 7th Street, next door to the Casanave Coffee Importing Co. Another brother had property on 8th Street, between Main and Los Angeles Streets. After a year spent in El Monte, we settled on a bee ranch in Los Flores Canyon. We lived there for four or five years. This later became the "Briggs" Property in La Crescenta. There was a spring on this property with a pool where the children could bathe. Then we went to Glendale (it was called Tropico where we lived) on property between the Los Angeles River and San Fernando Road. (This later became the first location of Lockheed.) The girls went to school there. The teacher, Minnie Bayright, boarded with us. Later she married our son, James. Colonel Griffith was a neighbor who lived in Verduga Canyon.*
>
> *There were no street cars in Los Angeles then. We visited my husband's brother who had ten acres located between the Los Angeles River and the present location of the Old Southern Pacific Depot. It was covered with willows. The Spanish people held celebrations near there. We watched them race horses and spear rings as the horses ran. They had beautiful silver-mounted saddles and bridles.*

Children attended some parties at the Griffith home. One day Col. Griffith offered us some property he owned across the River, for twenty-five cents an acre. We did not have the money to buy it. Later it was donated to the City of Los Angeles for a Park. It was named Griffith Park. Our youngest daughter, Pinky, age six, died when we were living in Los Flores Canyon (Dunsmore).

After a number of years we moved to Antelope Valley. Our eldest children were married and we had only our two youngest ones (Emma, called Birdie, and William) with us. We took a timber-culture Claim. On that claim I helped clear 30 acres of land and I ploughed it myself. Then we dug a well. My husband filled the bucket as we dug 140 feet and got water. We moved afterward to the town of Lancaster where we became Postmaster and Postmistress, which offices we held for fifteen years.

After 15 years we retired and bought a home in Santa Monica. My husband died there. My later years were occupied with activities in the Relief Corp, the Girls of '61 to '65 and the Rebeccas.

After Frank died in 1915, Hattie applied for a widow's pension and received twenty-five dollars per month. Hattie went to live with her daughter Birdie (Emma) and her family; she was active in several relief and Civil War organizations. She died in Los Angeles on September 20, 1926, and is buried in Evergreen Cemetery in Los Angeles next to Frank. Their names live on in the Crescenta Valley.

Frank and Hattie's monument in the family plot at Evergreen Cemetery, Los Angeles.

5

The Hall Family

Thomas Spencer Hall was one of the very first settlers in La Cañada, filing for a land patent in 1874. His property was federal land above the Rancho La Cañada land grant. By all accounts, he came to Los Angeles in 1873. He was born on August 20, 1826, in Norfolk, St. Lawrence County, New York, the youngest of six sons of Erastus Hall and Elizabeth Jackson Hall.

Education

Hall attended Yale College sporadically, probably due to financial concerns. He subsequently graduated from Vermont State Agricultural College in 1850 and read law with Bishop Perkins, a lawyer in Ogdensburg, New York. In 1852, he went to California, where he worked in a telegraph office and then practiced law. He did not have a law degree, which was not absolutely necessary in those days, especially in the West. According to the Yale Manuscripts and Archives:

> *Thomas S. Hall is listed as a freshman in the Class of 1850. He lived in New Haven at 1 Grove Street, and his home address was Raymondsville, NY. He is not listed in the 1847–48 catalog. He is also listed as a freshman in the catalog of 1845–46. At that time he lived on campus in North Middle College, also known as Berkeley Hall (1801–95).*

> *Statistics of the Class of 1850 of Yale College, New Haven, 1853: Thomas S. Hall, of Raymondsville, N.Y.; born at Norfolk, St. Lawrence Co., N.Y. Aug. 20, 1826; entered Freshman from Class of 1849, Oct. 1846; left College in summer of 1847; entered, and was graduated at the Vermont University, 1850, studied Law in Ogdensburg, N.Y., in the office of Bishop Perkins, Esq., 1851; went to California, 1852, where he is now engaged in a telegraph office; intends to practice Law as a profession.*

The General Catalogue of the University of Vermont and State Agricultural College, Burlington, Vermont, 1791–1900 (Burlington Free Press, 1901) records:

> *Thomas Spencer Hall, AM.M. 1858; and La Cañada, Cal., 26 March 1898; fr Yale Oct. 1847; fr Ramondsville, N.Y.: lawyer; pr Sonora, Cal; Potsdam, N.Y.; mfg. 70---; fruit grower at La Cañada;*
> *Capt 82 NY Vols 61; major Jan 62; Vols 61; major Jan 62; Col Dec 62-June 63".*

The *Catalogue of the Sigma Phi* (1891) notes:

> *Thomas Spencer Hall, La Cañada, Los Angeles County, Cal.*
> *Entered from Raymondsville, New York, A.B.1851, A.M. 1858*
> *Counsellor at Law, and fruit grower.*
> *Practiced at Sonora, Cal., until a short time before the Civil War; subsequently resided at Potsdam & Raymondsville, New York, where he was engaged in Manufacturing 1870 ----; then removed to California and engaged in his present business being as a Fruit-grower and Wine-grower, at La Cañada.*
> *Captain Co. E, 92nd Regt., N.Y., Vol. Inf'y, Oct. 10, 1861; Major Jan. 29, 1862; Colonel, Dec, 27, 1862: discharged, Colonel, June 1. 1863; commissioned Colonel Aug. 8. 1863 (e).*

Hall had several occupations. In the early 1850s, he was a telegraph operator and lawyer in Sonoma, California. In 1870, he was married, living in Norfolk, St. Lawrence County, New York, and was a custom miller. In 1880, the family was living in Los Angeles, and he was listed as a bookkeeper. He was also an internal revenue agent and customs broker for the government. He worked at this last profession until about 1889. Additionally, he was a notary public in Los Angeles, as well as a fruit and grape grower in La Cañada.

Marriage

On May 20, 1856, Hall married Catherine Sheldon Dearborn, who was born on January 1, 1828, in Madrid, St. Lawrence County, New York. Her parents were Samuel Dearborn and Caroline Sheldon. The Dearborns were a noted Revolutionary War family. Catherine and Thomas had four children, all born in New York. One son died before they moved to California. Their daughter Mary, born in 1860, died in Los Angeles before 1890. Their other sons were Tom and Sam.

Civil War

Hall enlisted in the Civil War at Potsdam, New York, on October 10, 1861, and was mustered in on October 30, 1861, as a captain in the Ninety-second New York Infantry. He was promoted to major on January 10, 1862. He was serving under General George B. McClellan when his son Thomas was born. He gave Tom the middle name McClellan. McClellan was an interesting figure in the Civil War; many consider him a failure, but he was highly respected by his men, as he did not send them needlessly into battle.

Colonel Thomas Spencer Hall during the Civil War, with his slouch hat. *Courtesy of the Morrisville State College Library.*

The following is an excerpt from the *Norwood News* on March 29, 1898, regarding Hall's Civil War service:

> *Mr. Hall gained an enviable reputation for the thoughtful care of his men, and his vigor, coolness and bravery in action. At the memorable battle of Fair Oaks, Col. Hall's regiment was called upon to perform such active work that 47 per cent of the regiment were reported killed or wounded.*

Union New York Volunteers
*92nd Regiment, New York Infantry [*below is only what applies to Hall's term of service]
Organized at Potsdam, N.Y., and mustered in January 1, 1862. Left State for Washington, D.C., March 5, 1862. Attached to 3rd Brigade, 3rd Division, 4th Army Corps, Army of the Potomac, to June, 1862.
Service. Advance on Manassas, Va., March 10–15, 1862. Ordered to the Peninsula, Virginia, March 28. Siege of Yorktown April 5–May 4. Reconnaissance toward Lee's Mills April 29. Battle of Williamsburg May 5. Operations about Bottom's Bridge May 21–23. Near Seven Pines May 29–30. Battle of Seven Pines or Fair Oaks May 31–June 1.
Something about the Ninety-second and Its Colonel.
Correspondence of the Evening Journal.
Potsdam, St. Lawrence co., Jan. 16, 1863.
The Ninety-Second.—The Potsdam Courier *of the 12th, says that T.S. Hall, late major of the 92d, who was mustered out when the regiment was consolidated has received a commission as colonel from Governor Seymour. The regiment has been placed upon its original footing of ten companies, and we understand is to be filled up with conscripts.*

He was honorably discharged on January 10, 1863, served as a major and made brevet colonel at discharge.

Moving to California

In the May 20, 1976 *La Cañada Valley Sun Centennial* issue, a short article about Hall states that he took a clipper ship around the Horn on his first visit to California in 1850 and that the family traveled on the Union Pacific Railway when they came to California.

The family was in Los Angeles by 1873. Like many early pioneers, Hall worked and lived in the city of Los Angeles and developed his La Cañada ranch on the weekends and in his spare time. When his sons Tom and Sam graduated from school in Los Angeles, they moved to the ranch full time. Assessor's records indicate that the current dwelling on the ranch property was built in 1890, but it was probably built earlier. Voter registrations provide valuable information on early pioneers, including their physical descriptions. Hall's physical description from the 1896 voter

The Hall Ranch in 1876. *Courtesy of La Cañada Congregational Church.*

registration, La Cañada Precinct, Los Angeles County, California, was five-foot-eight, dark complexion, blue eyes and gray hair.

Hall was very involved in the local Frank Bartlett Post No. 6 of the Grand Army of the Republic; they met every Tuesday evening at Good Templar's Hall on North Main Street. In 1883, he was post commander and aide-de-camp to the commander in chief.

Catherine died suddenly at the ranch on February 1, 1884. The following announcement is from the *Los Angeles Herald*, dated February 2, 1884:

> *Wife of Thomas Spencer Hall. Died February 1,884 in La Cañada. We regret to announce the sudden death of the esteemed wife of Colonel T.S. Hall, who died yesterday at their beautiful home in La Cañada.*

It is interesting to note that it does not mention her given name, only his name. It has always been thought that Catherine refused to live at the ranch. The family lived in Los Angeles, and Thomas did not move to the ranch full time until he retired in 1889, five years after Catherine's death.

There is no record of her death at the Los Angeles County Recorder's Office, and she was most likely buried at the ranch. On the same day he reported her death to the *Herald*, Hall submitted his rain report to the paper as well.

When Hall retired and moved to the ranch full time, he applied for and received an invalid (old age) pension for his Civil War service in 1890. They raised fruit crops, established a vineyard and winery, raised bees and harvested timber.

Hall obtained several different tracts of land from land patents, lumber patents, railroad land and surplus land from the State of California. His property holdings were estimated at one thousand acres. Records at the Los Angeles County Recorder's Office in Norwalk, California, list certificates for three patents on November 15, 1881, a State of California patent issued on July 2, 1886, and a federal patent issued on January 21, 1890.

Some of the land was acquired to obtain water rights and timber harvesting permits. The Halls operated the Hall Water Company, which supplied water to the residents below their property from Hall-Beckley Canyon. Descanso Gardens in La Cañada Flintridge today obtains at least 60 percent of its water from Hall-Beckley Canyon.

Thomas Spencer Hall died on March 24, 1898, at 225 North Hill, Los Angeles. The cause of death was valvular heart disease. Research has not been successful in determining what sort of dwelling or hospital was at 225 North Hill, but at the time of Hall's death, he owned only a vacant lot in Los Angeles, so it was not his home. He may have been boarding there, however, as there was a five-dollar boarding fee listed in his will. His obituary was in the *Los Angeles Times* on March 27, 1898:

> *Death of a Veteran*
> *Funeral of Col. Thomas Spencer Hall will be held today. Col. Thomas Spencer Hall, whose death occurred in this city, last Thursday* [March 24, 1898], *had an honorable record in the Civil War. He enlisted early in the war in the Ninety-second New York Volunteer Infantry, serving as captain until after of the battle of Fair Oaks, when by the loss of the superior officers he commanded the regiment. He came to Los Angeles twenty-five years ago. For several years he was Internal Revenue Collector, and subsequently spent much of him time on his ranch at La Cañada. All of his family died before him except two sons, now residents of La Cañada. For several years his health had been failing, and he finally passed away at the age of 72 years.*

His remains will be buried from the undertaking parlors of Orr & Hines, on Broadway, between Sixth and Seventh, at 1 o'clock today. Having been one of the early commanders of the old Bartlett Post of the Grand Army, it is expected that his comrades will attend the funeral in large numbers. The interment will be at Evergreen Cemetery. The Veteran Band is asked to attend.

Evergreen Cemetery is located at 204 North Evergreen Avenue in Los Angeles, California. It is in the Boyle Heights area between East First Street and Cesar Chavez Avenue (formerly Brooklyn Avenue). He is in Section G, Lot 84, in a single-plot grave. No one else is buried with him. There is a Civil War monument for him.

According to the Los Angeles Superior County Probate File No. 2510, dated April 23, 1898:

In the Last will and testament dated Feb. 3. 1891, the attorney was Will D. Gould, a prominent Los Angeles attorney with land holdings in the Crescenta Valley and after whom Gould Avenue in La Cañada is named. Hall's executors were his two sons, Thomas McClellan & Samuel Sheldon, both residing in La Cañada, California.

To Thomas McClellan Hall, my gold watch and chain, and all of my mules, live stock, harnesses, wagons and agricultural and horticultural implements of every description.

To my son, Samuel Sheldon Hall, my piano.

I give, bequeath and devise all the rest, residue and remainder of my personal and real estate, of every name and nature whatsoever, to my sons, Thomas McClellan Hall and Samuel Sheldon Hall, share and share alike.

His court-appointed estate appraisers were Theodor Pickens, Ivar A. Weid (GAR Frank Bartlett Post No. 6) and C.F. Heingeman (Los Angeles druggist). Appraisal was as follows:

Real Estate
Cash on land in Bank—$246.32
Cash received from rents of Broadway property—$300
290 [later corrected to 391] *acres of land in the County of Los Angeles, and being a part of Rancho La Cañada, together with water rights—$30,000.*
Lot in the City of Los Angeles fronting 60 feet on west side of Broadway between First and Franklin Streets—$18,000.
Blocks 3 South Santa Monica, Los Angeles County @ $200 each —$600

In Riverside County: An undivided one-half interest in and so the S.W. ¼ of the N.E. ¼, and the S.E. ¼ of the N.W. ¼, and the S.E ¼ of the S.W. ¼ of Sec. 26, T.4.S.R. 26, S.B. M being timber land—$400.
Personal Property
Farm implements—$20
Household furniture & jewelry—$100
Three (3) mules @ $50 each—$150
Lot 19 Block II of the Masonic Cemetery belonging to Los Angeles Lodge of F. and A. Masons No. 42, said lot being 10'x16'—no value listed
Total appraisal—$49,816.32

Like many of these old records, the file is not complete. Tom and Sam had to secure a $6,000.00 mortgage to settle the debts of the estate. The vacant lot on Broadway had been rented for $75.00 per month. The probate was closed on August 12, 1899, and the final accounting included expenses of $15.00 for the three estate appraisers, hay from Los Angeles Hay Storage & Milling, barley and bran from Excelsior Mills, alfalfa hay from Star Dairy and $128.00 for twelve pairs of white gloves. A further asset was listed as twenty-five puncheons (84-gallon casks) of wine, being 3,750 gallons at $0.15 a gallon, with a total value of $562.50.

Thus ended the life of an honorable, hardworking man. There were no fights over his estate and no lawsuits. He was honored and respected by his peers. He left a lasting legacy in the Crescenta Valley with Hall-Beckley Canyon, Winery Canyon and one of the last two remaining nineteenth-century ranches in the valley.

Samuel Sheldon Hall

Samuel Sheldon Hall was named after his maternal grandparents, Samuel Dearborn and Caroline Sheldon. Sam, as he was called, came to Los Angeles with his family in 1873 when he was four years old. He was educated at schools in Los Angeles and after graduation moved to the Hall Ranch in La Cañada full time, where he worked the ranch with his brother Tom. Samuel never married, loved music and had a full, active social life.

He was born in July 1869 in Norfolk, New York, the youngest child of Thomas Spencer Hall and Catherine Sheldon Dearborn. In addition to his brother Tom, he had an older brother who died in New York and a sister, Mary, who died before 1890. He did not attend college or serve in the military. His mother died in 1884, and his father died in 1898, leaving the ranch to Sam and his brother Tom equally. He loved music and played the piano at many social events in the valley.

Sometime after 1904, Sam left La Cañada and moved to Pasadena, where he lived for the rest of his life. He sold two separate properties to his brother Tom on November 10, 1904. This was four months after Tom's marriage.

Sam was extremely active in the Pasadena Elks Lodge #672, was a delegate to the National Convention and was a piano player and musical director at the lodge. It appears there was an Elks Lodge in La Cañada for a while that Sam and Tom helped organize. Sam had a long friendship and business relationship with Wesley W. Whitney, a part-time resident in La Cañada. Sam and Whitney operated a billiard establishment in Pasadena and later a chicken ranch on Colorado Boulevard.

Samuel Sheldon Hall died on January 25, 1929, in Altadena after a long illness following an operation. While Sam did move away from the valley, he was a member of a prominent pioneer family and was an active member of the local community for almost thirty years.

Thomas McClellan Hall

Thomas McClellan Hall was one of the few early pioneers who stayed in the valley. He did not move to Pasadena, the Arroyo Seco, other foothill communities or to Los Angeles. He was born while his father was serving in the Civil War under General George B. McClellan. Thomas was obviously very proud of his middle name, as he always used the abbreviation "McC" as his middle initial. This has caused name confusion in many records. In his youth, he was called T-Mac, but later in life he was always referred to as Tom.

Tom was born on March 31, 1862, in Norfolk, New York, the second child of Thomas Spencer Hall and Catherine Sheldon Dearborn. He was a fruit rancher, raised bees, maintained a vineyard, operated the Hall Water Company and the Hall Winery and was a part-time deputy sheriff and forest ranger.

He was eleven years old when his family came to Los Angeles in 1873. His father purchased land in La Cañada and developed it in his spare time. Tom was educated at schools in Los Angeles. After graduation, he moved to the Hall Ranch in La Cañada full time.

A Sunday afternoon at the Hall Ranch in 1900. *Top row, from left*: Samuel Hall, unknown, Tom Hall and unknown. On the right, peeking out from under a tree is Charles Pate. *Courtesy of La Cañada Congregational Church.*

The Hall Ranch in the 1880s and '90s was a hub for male social gatherings in the valley—no doubt due to the fact that Tom and Sam were bachelors and that there was a winery on the premises where wine could be easily purchased. They played cards, organized hunting parties and were trailblazers in the Angeles National Forest and the Arroyo Seco. According to Charles Pate, they called themselves the "Coyotes." It was likely not a den of debauchery, however, as Tom's aunt Sarah lived with the Hall family for over forty years until her death in 1916.

The 1896 voter registration for Sepulveda (Glendale School District) describes Tom as a farmer, age thirty-four, five-foot-eight, with a dark complexion, brown eyes, brown hair and a scar on his chin.

In 1898, Tom's father, Thomas Spencer Hall, died, and his estate and properties were split between Tom and his brother Sam. Tom and Sam divided 391 acres, with Tom taking the eastern half, including the Hall-Beckley Canyon, a large tract of the foothills on the north and as far south as Olive Lane on Alta Canyada (formerly Burr Avenue). In the 1900 census, Tom, Sam, Aunt Sarah, Theodore Pickens and a servant were living at the ranch.

From left: Tom and Hanna Hall with their German-born friend Rheinhold Guderian and his wife, Lina. Early 1900s. *Courtesy of the La Cañada Congregational Church.*

Tom was forty-two when he married Hanna W. Colberg on July 20, 1904, at Trinity Lutheran Church in Pasadena. Hanna was twenty-seven and was born in Pomerania, Germany. Her family immigrated to Iowa about 1895. Sometime before 1900, she moved to California, and in the 1900 census, she was working as a maid in Pasadena. Hanna's younger sister, Martha, later moved to California, married Chris Skow in 1917 and settled in La Cañada. Hanna lived to be ninety-nine years old, dying on February 9, 1976; she had been living with her daughter, Violet Cravens, in Hermosa Beach. She is buried in Forest Lawn Cemetery in Glendale, California.

Ever the romantic, Tom took his bride deer hunting for two weeks in Big Tujunga Canyon for their honeymoon. According to the *Los Angeles Times* of August 15, 1904, "Mr. & Mrs. Tom Hall and Ben Mendes returned from a two weeks deer hunt in Big Tujunga yesterday. The party killed five bucks and Mrs. Hall shot a large catamount."

Hanna at least got a nice dance in their honor after they got back, as reported in the *Los Angeles Times* of August 28, 1904:

> *Out of Town Society—La Cañada*
> *La Cañada Valley Club gave a dance at its hall Friday evening in honor of Mr. and Mrs. Tom Hall, who recently returned from their honeymoon in the Big Tujunga.*

Tom and Hanna had one child, a daughter, Violet H., born on December 3, 1905. She married Donald D. Waggoner and had two daughters, Lauris and JoAnn. Later, she married Curtis Cravens. Violet died in 1993 in San Diego County. She contributed to the *La Cañada Valley Sun Centennial* issue in 1976, writing a long article entitled "Folksy Memories of La Canyada." Her comments are quoted throughout this chapter.

Four months after Tom's marriage, his brother Sam sold him two properties and moved to Pasadena, leaving Tom the sole owner of the Hall Ranch property and winery and the Hall Water Company.

"In the West, Whiskey Is for Drinking and Water Is for Fighting Over"

The story of the lack of water and efforts to secure enough water in the valley could fill a book. Ranchers who controlled canyon water formed individual water companies, whether official or not. Even today, the city of La Cañada Flintridge has four water companies. Water in the valley was a constant source of concern, and Tom grew weary of the situation, as noted in the following article from the *Los Angeles Times* of June 21, 1905:

> *La Cañada*
> *Water Complications.*
> *La Cañada, June 20. The water supply here, which has long been a serious question in the summer time, has taken a new aspect. Tom Hall, who owns the major part of the Hall water system, has refused to sell any water during the summer unless the buyers incorporate their interests, put in new conduits, water boxes, etc. Mr. Hall says that under existing conditions he sells a man at the lower end of the valley water and during the day the buyer comes steaming up asking why the water is not coming, and usually it proves to be a break or some accidental turning off by some members above the persons supposed to be using the water.*
>
> *This quibbling has become obnoxious to Hall, and to better conditions he requires an incorporation and a regular schedule, to be arranged by the usual buyers.*
>
> *This is not the only complication regarding the water question here. The La Cañada Land and Water Company has a suit pending, and the La Cañada Water Company one also, which will probably be set for trial soon. In both of these cases W.C. Cohen, owner of the "Gould's Castle," is the*

Taming the water in Hall-Beckley Canyon. It supplies much of the water for Descanso Gardens in La Cañada Flintridge. *Courtesy of the La Cañada Congregational Church.*

plaintiff. If he wins and the Hall system does not come up to a business basis and incorporate, about four hundred acres of orange and lemon trees will be in a critical condition.

Hunting

If there was one thing Tom Hall had a passion for, it was hunting. In the 1880s and '90s, he had his group of so-called Coyotes and also family friend Theodor Pickens as hunting companions, and let's not forget that he took his wife hunting on their honeymoon. The Hall Ranch, being inhabited by bachelors, was a perfect meeting place for the hunters. While a lot of the hunting was done in Big Tujunga Canyon, Tom did venture elsewhere, as recounted by his daughter Violet:

When hunting season came, everything stopped! He [hired hand Ben] *took the pack animals and went ahead to the "big mountains," the Iron Mountain area that overlooks Acton, and set up camp. My father would follow and they would hunt for a couple of weeks.*

According to the *Los Angeles Times* of July 10, 1897, "Tom Hall and Mr. Pickens have gone far back into the mountains on their annual hunting trip after grizzlies and things."

On July 6, 1899, the *Los Angeles Times* printed the following article:

Hunting a Honey-Thief
Crescenta Cañada Nimrods in Pursuit of a Large Bear.
The people of Crescenta Cañada have had a bear scare during the last few days. A Large female bruin, accompanied by a cub, has been driven by hunger to the foothills, where she has been preying on the bee ranches near the mouth of the Arroyo Seco Canyon. One bee man reports $300 or $400 damages among his bee stands. A party of hunters consisting of Tom and Sam Hall and Kirk Reynolds, and under the leadership of old "Dad" Perkins (Pickens), a celebrated bear-slayer, has gone in pursuit of the honey-thief. Persons who have seen the footprints of the old she bear have inferred that she is an enormous animal. This inference has been fully confirmed by the hunters who came across her in the mountains the other night, but deferred attack on account of the darkness. Although of immense

size, the bear is very lean on account of the scarcity of food. A young Englishman who was camping in Arroyo Seco Canyon forsook his shack several days ago and moved to the valley, owing to the proximity of the bear.

On September 25, 1907, the *Los Angeles Herald* reported:

Police Commissioner Leaves to Hunt Deer
Special to the Herald.
Pasadena, Sept. 24—Police Commissioner W.D. Medill starts for the hills tomorrow morning early with Tom Hall of La Cañada to hunt deer. They will be gone for several days and in the meantime their friends will whet their appetites for venison.

A Question of Judgment

Tom's daughter Violet recounted that he spoke Spanish very well and was the deputy sheriff in the valley for the Mexican community. She remembers often being awakened in the middle of the night with the request that "Mr. Tom" was needed.

A killing occurred in 1907 involving a former employee of Tom's, Jesus Verdugo. The newspapers stated that he was the son of Don Teodoro Verdugo. Tom was the deputy sheriff who tracked and captured the accused murderer, Benito Menillies. The following account is a compilation of newspaper articles in the *Los Angeles Herald* and the *Los Angeles Times*. The articles all went into the extensive history of Don Teodoro Verdugo and had various spellings of Menillies's name. It should be noted that while Teodoro had fourteen children, there is no record of him having a son named Jesus, and the criminal Verdugo was too old to be the son of Teodoro. According to the *Los Angeles Herald* of March 17, 1907, "The men engaged in the fight are all said to have been drinking. Verdugo's assailants are said to have reputations as bad men at the camp." The *Times* and *Herald* reported:

Knife Wounds Are Fatal to Spanish Don
Jesus Verdugo Dies of Injuries
Jesus Verdugo, son of the late Don Theodore Verdugo, died at 3 o'clock yesterday afternoon as a result of knife wounds received in a fight with Beneto Menillies and Juan Juarnitas at the grading camp near La Cañada, where

Verdugo was foreman, late Saturday night. Menillies was arrested a few hours later in Verdugo canyon, where he was hiding, by Deputy Sheriff Tom Hall and Forest Ranger H.E. White of Pasadena and was brought to the county jail at Los Angeles. He will be charged with the murder of Verdugo.

According to acquaintances of the men concerned, Menillies was enraged at Verdugo, whom he blamed because he had been docked for time lost.

The men met a short distance from the camp and talked. Witnesses say Menillies suddenly sprang upon Verdugo and bore him to the ground, at the same time plunging a large hunting knife into the foreman's breast. During the fight Verdugo succeeded in drawing his own knife and inflicted severe cuts upon Menillies.

Menillies arose from the prostrate form of the foreman and went to a cabin he owned near La Cañada. There he obtained his rifle and two dogs and went directly to Verdugo canyon. He was hiding in a thick underbrush when captured…

A tell-tale trail of blood led to the capture of Beneto Menillies in Verdugo Canyon, last night. He is now held in the County Jail on the charges of having murdered Jesus Verdugo in a fight Saturday night at the grading camp of the la Cañada Valley Railway. The camp is about four miles east of Pasadena.

According to reliable informants, Jesus Verdugo is the son of Don Verdugo and at one time he was a trusted employee of Deputy sheriff Tom Hall, who trailed and captured his murderer.

Into the very heart of what was once the domain of the father of the man he is accused of killing, Menillies was trailed. The drops of blood afforded the officer a clear trail for a considerable portion of the distance. Out in the wild undergrowth of the canyon the officer found the wounded man, who offered no resistance.

In one of those too-often-questionable verdicts, Benito was found not guilty. The *Los Angeles Times* of June 14, 1907, reported:

Mexican Freed

After Being Out Nearly Four Hours, Jury Finds Menillies Not Guilty of Murder.

After being out nearly four hours the jury in the case of Beneto Menillies, on trial for the murder of Jesus Verdugo March 16, 1907, in Verdugo Canyon, brought in a verdict of not guilty at 9:20 o'clock last night.

The two Mexicans quarreled, while in a woodcutters' camp together, and Verdugo was fatally stabbed. Menillies's defense was that Verdugo had struck at him with a knife, and that he had struck back in self defense.

Testimony dealt largely with the nature of the two men, as to the peacefulness, and the dead man was given rather the better character.

In the pocket of Verdugo, according to testimony taken yesterday, his knife was found, the blades closed, sticky with his own blood which had soaked through his clothes.

Now, this would just be an interesting story of something that happened to Tom Hall while he was deputy sheriff except for the fact that Tom subsequently hired Benito Menillies to work and live on his ranch for many years. We find him living at the Hall Ranch in the 1910 and 1920 censuses. Daughter Violet writes about "Ben" quite affectionately:

Ben was an Indian who came to work for us on the ranch. He was born on the Indian reservation in Riverside and did many jobs for us.

Not having any playmates, I followed Ben and my Dad around like a shadow. I had dolls but preferred the animals. Ben brought me two baby skunks once and I raised them to half grown when they mysteriously disappeared—I think my mother had something to do with it.

As soon as I was big enough to hold a .22 rifle, Ben taught me to shoot. I used to hunt squirrels and rabbits. I also hunted from my horse. I had a saddle holster and Ben trained me not to be gun shy. We had a mountain lion in the canyon, and Ben had seen his tracks and hunted him so everyone was on the alert. Ben finally tracked him down, and we had a rug made with the pelt and head and claws still intact.

Hall Winery

Tom was interviewed by Grace Overbeck for her 1938 book, *A History of La Crescenta and La Cañada Valleys* and they discussed the winery. The first grapevines were planted on the ranch in 1884, and when the grapes matured, a recently constructed barn was used for a winery. According to Tom, "Tourists were driving through in 'buggies' and stopped to sample the wine; nearly all the sampling resulted in orders to be sent C.O.D. to the homes in the East, and thus a flourishing industry was established."

An old-timer's account in the *Crescenta Valley Ledger* states: "On payday, the local Mexican workers would all rush up to the Hall ranch to fill their jugs of wine." These statements contradict most accounts that the Halls only sold

A modern-day picture of the Hall barn. On the slope where there are now deodar pines, there used to be grapevines.

wine in bulk to wineries in Los Angeles. Legal or not, they probably had a small bottling operation at the ranch.

Not too long after Tom's marriage in 1904, he discontinued operating the winery and just sold his grapes in bulk to local wineries. There is a story that Tom Hall's wife, Hanna, was a teetotaler and sometimes put vinegar in the wine to get him to stop selling it. Whether this is true, no one knows; maybe his wine just went bad sometimes, and his wife got blamed for it. Or maybe she got tired of all the people running up there all the time to buy wine. After his marriage, Tom's brother Sam moved to Pasadena, leaving Tom with a new family and sole responsibility for the ranch, winery and water company, as well as the job of part-time deputy sheriff. Closing the winery operation reduced his burden and was probably quietly welcomed by Tom.

Hall Ranch

The original Hall Ranch, also known as Alta Canyada, was pioneered by Tom's father, Thomas Spencer Hall, who purchased several land patents, state land and railroad land, reportedly totaling 1,000 acres. Initially, he planted citrus groves and later, in 1884, grapevines. The properties were not all connected, and some were purchased to obtain water rights and timber harvesting permits. When Thomas S. Hall died in 1898, he left an estate of 391 acres equally divided between sons Tom and Sam. Tom acquired two tracts of land from his brother Sam in 1904, as well as additional land patents in 1908 and 1910.

Much has been written claiming that Tom sold five hundred acres of his property to Edwin T. Earl in 1913 for the development of the Alta Canyada housing tract. In my research at the Los Angeles County Recorder's Office, I found no record in the deed index books for 1912, 1913 or 1914 of any sale from Hall to Earl. There is one record dated April 2, 1914, from Thomas McClellan Hall to the Lanterman Estate. What the Lanterman Estate's involvement was in this transaction or with E.T. Earl is not known, but it had real estate interests and maybe acted as a broker.

The November 1933 fire and New Year's Day mudslide of 1934, combined with the Depression that caused many valley ranchers to go bankrupt, devastated Tom. His beloved foothills were ravaged by nature. Heartbroken and almost seventy-two, too old to keep struggling to maintain the ranch and with no one to take it over, he filed a default of mortgage notice to the Security Bank in February 1934, leaving the ranch in October.

The property passed through at least three owners, but a 68.8-acre parcel of the original Hall Ranch and the 1890 winery barn and house located at the intersection of Alta Canyada and Hacienda are still intact. The current owners have owned the ranch since 1947. The property includes Winery Canyon and the Winery Canyon Debris Basin.

After leaving the ranch, Tom and Hanna moved in with Hanna's sister and brother-in-law, Martha and Chris Skow, at 4874 Commonwealth Avenue in La Cañada. Tom and Hanna lived there for several years. In February 1944, failing health required Tom to enter St. Erne Sanitarium in Inglewood. He died there on September 15, 1947, due to complications of old age. He was cremated, and there is no record of a probate filing at the Hall of Records.

A very warm obituary was written by Bea Snoke for the *Crescenta Valley Ledger* on Thursday, September 18, 1947, although it is a little difficult to separate what Tom did and what his father originally started:

> *La Cañada Pioneer Tom Hall Dies at 83; Funeral Set Today*
> *Death claimed another Valley pioneer when Thomas McClellan Hall (Tom) passed away on Monday afternoon, September 15, at an Inglewood Sanitarium where he has been in failing health for several years. He was 83 years old. He is*

survived by his widow, Hannah Colbert Hall [sic], *who resides on New York avenue, in Altadena; a daughter, Violet, now Mrs. Curtis Craven of Hermosa Beach and her two grown daughters, Lauris and JoAnn Waggoner.*

The funeral will be held today, Thursday, September 18, at three p.m. at Kieffer and Eyerick Mortuary on Harvard in Glendale.

Long time residents of La Cañada will recall Tom as one of the outstanding characters of his time. His father, Col. Hall (who had served under Gen. McClellan in the Civil War) had brought his family, a wife, two sons and a daughter here seeking healthful climatic conditions for eldest son, Tom, who responded so satisfactorily that when the father died during March, 1898 the sons, Sam and Tom, divided the large acreage and Tom took the eastern half including the Hall-Beckley Canyon, a large tract of the foothills on the north and as far south as Olive lane on Alta Canyada road.

The original Hall ranch house was located near what is now the Charles Arnt property. Later, young Tom built a house near what is now called Alta Canyada road and still later moved it to its present location on Linda Vista not far from the present Dennis Morgan property. About 15 or 17 years ago the house changed hands and went to an Englishman named Cherriton who never lived here but sold it to the present owners. The 1933 fire and subsequent New Year's Day flood had taken their toll in more ways than one, and Tom and his wife went to live with Mr. and Mrs. Chris Skow on Commonwealth where they remained for about five years. Mrs. Skow (Martha) and Mrs. Hall are sisters, formerly of Iowa.

Much of the former Hall holdings were bought by the late E.T. Earl in 1913 and he is reported to have had planted here the fine deodars which now stand sentinel duty in fond memory of those departed. Much of this interesting information comes from Charles Pate who arrived on the scene about 1893 and became a life long friend of the Halls. From Mrs. Skow we learn that Tom first planted much of his tillable land to citrus groves, later changing to wine grapes. His hobby was hunting and he had some fine hounds and several horses. It was in 1904 that he met his future wife, Hannah, as she came to visit mutual friends of the two, and remained to be married in a Pasadena church.

When we first moved to Alta Canyada we used to walk around these hills, then sparsely settled, and Tom became our good friend and always genial advisor on all things local. Time marches on, and it's with deep sadness that we now record his passing, for he loved these hills and soil and almost seemed a part of them. The ravages of that fire and flood were heartbreaking to old Tom and he never recovered from that shock, for along with the destruction it also tore out his heart, and he couldn't make a comeback against those elements.

6

The Lanterman Family

No family or individual has left a more lasting legacy in La Cañada than the Lanterman family. From Jacob L. Lanterman to grandson Lloyd Lanterman, the family lived, worked and contributed to La Cañada for over 110 years.

Jacob Luce Lanterman, the co-founder of La Cañada, was born in New Jersey on April 8, 1827, the second child of Peter Lanterman and Rachel Diltz. He had five sisters and one brother. Jacob had taught school and saved his money to attend Baltimore Dental College, where he obtained his dental degree. The college was founded in 1840 and was the first dental school in the world. After graduation, he settled in rural Lansing, Michigan. He married Ammoretta Jane Crissman on May 17, 1856, in Rome, Michigan, and they had four children, one of whom died before they moved to California.

In 1875, Lanterman came to the valley, staying at Delia Dunks's Verdugo Heights resort and exploring options to settle in the area. He was joined by Colonel Adolphus W. Williams, a fellow Lansing resident. On December 16, 1875, Williams and Lanterman purchased Rancho La Cañada for $10,000. (The details of this partnership are recounted in chapter ten.)

Jacob did not practice dentistry after coming to California. He would have to have had a practice in Los Angeles to be successful, as the valley was scarcely populated in the 1870s. Besides developing his rancho property, Jacob had extensive farming operations, raising figs, raisins, lemons, navel oranges, apricots, grape vineyards, barley and also kept bees. In 1885, he was on the planning committee to establish the Pasadena Fruit Growers Association.

Jacob Lanterman on the porch at Homewood. *Courtesy of the Lanterman Museum Historical Foundation.*

The following is excerpted from *Greater Los Angeles and Southern California: Portraits and Personal Memoranda*, published in 1910:

> *Jacob L. Lanterman, La Cañada*
> *Born in New Jersey, 1827 died at Glendora, Cal., 1908. Reared as the son of a poor farmer in New Jersey. Secured an education by individual exertions and finally worked his way through the Baltimore Dental College, then went to Michigan and opened his office at Lansing, then a little bank woods settlement, but soon to be the state capital; as soon as practice would warrant married Ammoretta J. Crissman, who came from near his New Jersey home; four children born, one dying in infancy and three being now residents of Southern California, a competency realized from profession work, bank and farming, but at expense of his health. Dr. Lanterman came to Los Angeles Co. in 1874, buying several thousand acres of wild land at La Cañada, which he transformed into the beautiful family home, known as Homewood. There his children, Stella, Frank and Roy, were reared, and there his wife died in 1902, he himself passed away at the home of his daughter, Mrs. Stella B. La Fetra, at Glendora in 1908—a man of sterling character, as quiet as his demeanor as in his charities.*

Jacob died on November 10 at his daughter Stella's home in Glendora. His obituary from the November 11, 1908 *Los Angeles Times* reads:

> *Jacob L. Lanterman, Father of Former Coroner, Dies at Daughter's Home in Glendora.*

Dr. Jacob L. Lanterman, father of former Coroner Dr. R.S. Lanterman, died yesterday afternoon at the home of his daughter, Mrs. L.M. LaFetra, in Glendora. He had been suffering since Sunday from a stroke of paralysis.

The elder Dr. Lanterman was a pioneer, coming to Southern California in 1874. He was 81 years old at the time of his death, and for several years had been in poor health. He leaves a daughter, Mrs. LaFetra, and two sons, Dr. Lanterman and Frank D. Lanterman.

Funeral services will be held tomorrow morning at 10:30 o'clock at the residence of Mrs. LaFetra in Glendora and at 1:30 o'clock in the afternoon at the chapel at Evergreen Cemetery, this city.

Ammoretta Jane Crissman and Pickens Canyon Water

Ammoretta Lanterman was born in Blairstown, New Jersey, in January 1831 to Jonas Crissman and Susan Snover. She had two brothers and four sisters. Ammoretta was an impressive woman who brought her own money to the marriage and participated in business dealings.

There is a rather silly story involving Ammoretta and the purchase of Pickens Canyon water from Theodor Pickens in 1878, a full accounting of which is told in chapter eight. The story goes that she tired of the water problem and back-and-forth dealings and rode up to Pickens's cabin in La Crescenta, where she threatened him with a gun until he sold her the water. The appeals trial provides the correct story. In fact, Pickens made a water rights deal with Jacob, and then Pickens rode down about a week later and sold the land to Ammoretta for $1,200, which she purchased along with forty acres in Section 21 with her separate wedding money. Putting the water rights in Ammoretta's name was a smart move on Jacob's part, as this was two months before the appeals trial started, and since the rights were not in Jacob's name, they could not be considered in the trial negotiations.

The Pickens Canyon water was transported to La Cañada by a gravity-flow system via redwood flumes in trestles to the northern boundaries of the rancho and then by concrete pipe to diversion boxes to each subscribed property owner, who held the twice-weekly delivered flow in small reservoirs on their properties. It operated as the La Cañada Land and Water Company, which was incorporated in 1892. There was resentment among La Crescenta

Ammoretta Crissman Lanterman, probably taken in Michigan. *Courtesy of the Lanterman Museum Historical Foundation.*

residents that their water was being supplied to La Cañada. It was also Ammoretta's idea to drill water wells on the east side of the rancho, near the arroyo; this was also successful.

In 1924, the La Cañada Irrigation District was formed, and it currently supplies approximately 40 percent of the city of La Cañada Flintridge's water supply. The district purchased the Lanterman Pickens Canyon water rights and owns the canyon, about seventy acres. It operates on a tunnel system of delivery, and La Crescenta is still providing water to La Cañada.

Ammoretta passed away on November 12, 1902, while staying at her son Frank's house at 120 East Adams Street in Los Angeles. She is buried at Evergreen Cemetery in the family plot.

STELLA BIRDELLA LANTERMAN

The oldest daughter, Stella, was born in Lansing, Michigan, on March 12, 1848. She married Lawson M. La Fetra in 1881, and they moved to Glendora, where they became successful farmers. They did not have any children. Lawson died in 1907, and Stella continued the farming operations. She eventually moved to Altadena and owned a twenty-room house at 1725 Foothill Boulevard in Altadena. She died on November 11, 1933, at her home. She and her husband are buried in the Lanterman family plot in Evergreen Cemetery.

Frank Dexter Lanterman

Born in Lansing, Michigan, on December 31, 1860, Frank Dexter was a civil engineer and surveyor and a graduate of the University of the Pacific. After graduation, he participated in the development of the Lanterman property, and his first job out of college was to further survey the property. He established the F.D. Lanterman Realty Company in Los Angeles to sell the rancho property.

Frank D. Lanterman and W.T. Somes formed Valley Water Company of La Cañada on October 1, 1910, and the "Lanterman Well" was drilled on Lanterman property. When electricity came to the valley around 1910 and made possible deep well pumping, the company was the first producer of a dependable well-water supply in the area. Frank D. was the first president of Valley Water Company; later, he became manager-secretary and served as secretary until his retirement in 1910. The Valley Water Company has continued in operation to the present day.

Frank's first wife was Hattie Fisher, and they had a daughter, Harriet. After Hattie's death, Frank married Mary Hills, and they had a daughter, Lulu (Johnson). Harriet was a prominent real estate agent in La Cañada for many years. Neither Harriet nor Lulu had any children. Frank died on May 16, 1940, and is buried in the family plot at Evergreen Cemetery.

Dr. Roy

Roy Stanley Lanterman, affectionately referred to by valley residents as Dr. Roy, was born on July 20, 1869, in Lansing, Michigan. He was quite young when the family moved to California. He attended high school in Glendale and in 1893 received his medical degree from Johns Hopkins in Baltimore, Maryland. He returned to Southern California and set up practice in Santa Monica, where he met his wife, Emily Folsom, the daughter of a prominent Santa Monica physician.

Roy and Emily married in Santa Monica on June 3, 1895. They received land in La Cañada as a wedding present and moved there after their marriage. Dr. Roy tried to combine doctoring and farming in the sparsely settled area. Emily Folsom was born in Washington, D.C., on December 10, 1873, and soon her family moved to Santa Monica. She was very social and

Seated are Dr. Roy and Emily, and standing are Lloyd and Frank Lanterman. *Courtesy of the Lanterman Museum Historical Foundation.*

disliked living in the isolated valley. Their first son, Lloyd Stanley, was born in La Cañada in 1897, but there were not enough people to have a profitable physician's practice, and wind, drought and freezes made farming difficult. They moved to Los Angeles in 1900, and Dr. Roy set up a medical practice.

Due to a political fluke more than anything, Dr. Roy was elected Los Angeles coroner in 1906, although he is not listed as coroner on the official website, perhaps because he did not serve very long. Dr. Roy was his own man. His wife, Emily, had been briefly married at age nineteen due to family pressure, and she quickly divorced. He was also criticized for being one of the few doctors who would treat prostitutes. He followed his conscience and not necessarily the rules of society. In 1906, Dr. Roy went to San Francisco to bring medical aid to San Francisco fire and earthquakes victims. He established the relief hospital there. His impressions from that time affected later decisions made in building his dream home.

The family moved back to La Cañada about 1914 and built their stately home on Verdugo Road, called El Retiro (the Retreat). By this time, automobile travel had made living in the valley much easier, and Dr. Roy opened a practice in Glendale, as well as the one at his home where he treated many loyal valley residents, some of whom were unable to pay, especially during the Depression. The original property was thirty-five acres, and he also had farming operations assisted by his two sons. Emily was very social and was involved in the community. She was a life member of La Cañada Thursday Club, twice serving as president, and she was also a charter member of the La Cañada Congregational Church, where she served as chairman of the Woman's Guild and as church historian. Their home in La Cañada was the center of social activity, and many plays were presented in the upstairs ballroom. Despite the large size of the home, Emily took care of it with only occasional domestic help.

Dr. Roy died on September 8, 1948, and Emily died at home on January 21, 1949. Both are buried in the family plot in Evergreen Cemetery. They had two sons, Frank Dexter and Lloyd Stanley.

Uncle Frank

Frank Dexter Lanterman was named for his uncle, probably because the senior Frank Dexter had no sons; this has caused confusion in some historical accounts, which have mixed them up at times. Our younger Frank D. was born in Los Angeles in 1901. When the family moved back to La Cañada in 1914, he attended Glendale High School and then the College of Music at the University of Southern California (USC), where he studied organ, piano and composition. He completed four years of study but did not graduate due to a dispute over his insistence on being absent to attend a musical event. However, he remained loyal to USC. He was a lifelong bachelor.

One of his first jobs was playing the organ at the Glendale Alexander Theatre (now the Alex Theatre) for four years. In 1928, he went to Melbourne, Australia, to become the organist at the new State Theatre, where he stayed for two years. The Lanterman Archives are in the process of transcribing all the letters he wrote home during this period. After returning to California, he continued his career as an organist for ten more years.

Demands of the Lanterman Estate increased after the death of his uncle Frank in 1940, and music became less important as he became more involved with the business operations, which involved many tracts of land in the valley that were being developed by the four cousins, Frank, Lloyd, Harriet and Lulu.

Water was a never-ending problem in the valley. The Municipal Water Act of 1911 only allowed water districts to be formed for municipalities. It was Frank's goal to get this amended and allow the valley to obtain Metropolitan Water District (MWD) water without having to annex to a municipality. He ran for and won his first term as a Republican state assemblyman with his main objective to get this act amended. Frank said, "We shouldn't have to annex to get water; we shouldn't let water be used for political purposes."

Orange County was also desirous of this change, and Frank coauthored amendments with Earl Stanley of Newport Beach. They were approved in April 1951 as an emergency measure. Eventually, progress was made, and the boundaries of the Foothill Water District were established. The district became a member of the MWD. In July 1955, new pipes supplying water to the valley brought a steady source of municipal water. The valley, which was already changing from rural to suburban, experienced rapid growth in residents due to the security of a permanent supply of water.

In 1955, Frank was named La Cañada's Citizen of the Year, and he and his family had a big write-up in the *La Cañada Valley Sun* on December 29, 1955. As often happens with hometown newspapers, they laid it on a little thick regarding Frank and his family's involvement with bringing water to the valley. He replied by writing a very gracious letter to the editor saying that no one person or family can take credit for the water supply in the valley and attempted to give credit where credit was due, especially to the early settlers who lived in the canyons and worked so hard to harvest the water.

Frank served fourteen terms as a state legislator—twenty-eight years—and was known for reaching across the aisle. He was called "Uncle Frank" by everyone. He mentored young politicians and helped pass many important legislative programs. When he retired in 1978, a long article in the *Los Angeles Times* ran with the headline: "State Assembly's Uncle Frank Retires; the People Lose a Voice."

Frank came back to La Cañada, dying at Glendale Adventist Hospital on April 27, 1981. He was cremated, and his ashes were placed in the family plot at Evergreen Cemetery. He was honored by the California State Assembly, as recounted in the May 8, 1981 *Los Angeles Times*:

> *Assembly Pays Final Tribute to Frank Lanterman*
> *Sacramento. The state Assembly paid an affectionate final tribute Thursday to former colleague Frank Lanterman, a champion of mental patients' rights who died last week.*
>
> *Lanterman, 78, spent 28 years in the assembly before retiring in 1978. A conservative Republican from La Cañada Flintridge, he was best known for sponsoring laws aimed at preventing unneeded hospitalization of the mentally ill and increasing aid to the programs.*
>
> *He was "The shepherd for the lost and the needy and the hopeless in our society," said Assemblyman Lawrence Kapiloff (D-San Diego) during an hour of speeches in praise of Lanterman.*
>
> *With Lanterman's brother, Lloyd, looking on from the podium, the Assembly passed a resolution hailing Lanterman, the son of a surgeon, as "A healer on a grand scale."*
>
> *A letter from President Reagan to Lloyd Lanterman, read during the tribute, mourned "the loss of a good friend."*

Lloyd Stanley

Totally different from his younger brother, Lloyd was a gentle soul. Lloyd was born in La Cañada in February 1897, and by 1900 the family had moved to Los Angeles, where he attended school. After the family moved back to La Cañada, he attended Glendale High School and then USC, where he obtained a degree in engineering.

Lloyd served briefly in World War I, assigned to one of the first U.S, military air squadrons. He served as a machinist and toolmaker stationed in Perris, California. He had a passion for steam engines and worked in this field as a consultant. He later became president of the Lanterman Estate

Corporation. He won national recognition as an automotive engineer in 1930 and 1932, when the racing cars he designed for the Harry A. Miller Company won the Indianapolis 500. In 1922, he designed an innovative steam generator, which he built and later patented.

Like his younger brother, he was a lifelong bachelor, but later in life he was engaged to Florence Pate, daughter of Charles Pate. When Pate came to the valley in 1893, he worked as an apricot picker for Lloyd's grandfather, Jacob Lanterman. Sadly, Florence died suddenly in March 1957 at the age of fifty-three.

Lloyd's younger brother Frank was the outgoing, boisterous brother, and easygoing Lloyd allowed him to make the family decisions. In 1969, a trust was set up in which the bulk of the brothers' estate was willed to their alma mater, USC, and the remainder to the La Cañada Congregational Church. After Frank's death in 1981, Lloyd started having second thoughts about leaving the estate, including the house, to USC. He was worried that he would not be allowed to live in the house, but more importantly, he feared that the family home would be torn down. Lloyd thought he might be able to leave the home to his church, but it could not afford to maintain it.

After many complicated transactions, Lloyd bought Frank's half interest in the house and estate from USC, paying the bulk in cash and thirty acres of land in Cherry Canyon. He turned the property over to the City of La Cañada Flintridge to preserve and maintain the premises for community and civic purposes, with the stipulation that he be allowed to live there until he died. Lloyd continued to live in the house with a caregiver, giving occasional informal tours to visitors. He died on February 5, 1997, at Verdugo Hills Hospital. He was cremated and is buried in the family plot at Evergreen Cemetery.

After Lloyd's passing, the city took over operation of the house. The original intent was to move the La Cañada City Hall there and also operate it as a community center. Neighbor opposition and other issues proved this to not be a practical option, and the city decided to preserve the house as a museum.

While there are no descendants remaining of Jacob and Ammoretta, there are many family legacies still here.

Homewood

After purchasing the rancho, Jacob and Ammoretta immediately set about to build a suitable family home, which they named Homewood. The original house was a three-room farmhouse plus a bath, a dining room, a parlor and a kitchen. In 1900, an expanded front-entry porch was added.

The house still stands at 1322 Verdugo Road near the La Cañada Congregational Church. After the deaths of Jacob and Ammoretta, it remained in the family, occupied by the F.D. Lanterman family until about 1940. For a while, it was a boardinghouse, and then it was sold about 1948. Since then, it has had several owners. In 1986, the current owner, a California state senator, purchased it. Over the years, it has been substantially updated, enlarged and remodeled and is much grander than the original residence.

Homewood in the late 1800s, facing Verdugo Road, before the 1900 porch expansion. The stone pillar was one of a pair that was torn down in 1984 because it was three feet into the sidewalk, which needed to be expanded for handicapped access. *Courtesy of the Lanterman Museum Historical Foundation.*

La Cañada Congregational Church

The original La Cañada Congregational Church at the intersection of Michigan Avenue (Foothill Boulevard) and Verdugo Road. *Courtesy of the Lanterman Museum Historical Foundation.*

Another lasting legacy of Jacob and Ammoretta is the La Cañada Congregational Church, which for many years was known as the Church of the Lighted Window; only recently was the name changed back to the La Cañada Congregational Church. In 1883, with no church or schoolhouse in the valley, several residents would meet at Jacob and Ammoretta's home, where they arranged informal religious services. In 1897, fifteen people met at the Lanterman home and drew up a statement of faith. Thus, they formally founded the La Cañada Congregation Church. Plans to build a church at the intersection of Foothill Boulevard and Verdugo Avenue were immediately put into effect. It was a one-story frame building. The Lantermans donated the land for the new church, and local residents contributed $1,200 in cash and labor. The formal dedication was on April 19, 1898; nearly two hundred people attended.

The original church was replaced in 1924 with the current church structure. The stained-glass lighted window at the front of the church was donated by the Lanterman family in memory of Jacob and Ammoretta. Grandson Frank Dexter was the organist at the new church building dedication. In 1969, the church was proclaimed a historic landmark of the State of California. The Lanterman family remained loyal members of the church their entire lives.

The Lanterman House (El Retiro)

Remembering his time in San Francisco after the 1906 earthquake, Dr. Roy and Emily Lanterman commissioned architect Arthur Haley to design a "fireproof mansion in the foothills." Their home at 4420 Encinas Drive is in the Craftsman style of the grand homes near where they lived in the Westmoreland district in Los Angeles. The house is U-shaped and two stories, with thirty-eight French doors and no front door. They had to put a doorbell by one of the French doors so people would know where to knock. It is 8,832 square feet, with the entire second floor a ballroom. A massive granite fireplace was built from stones from the property that is now Descanso Gardens.

As electricity was just reaching the valley, the house was state-of-the-art, fitted with both gas and electricity. The original home sat on 35.0 acres, but the current property is 1.2 acres. As Frank and Lloyd were bachelors, they never remodeled or changed anything, and the house is a trip back to 1914, Emily's aprons still hang in the kitchen. It contains some of Jacob and Ammoretta's furnishings from Homewood.

While the home was saved, when the city took over operation of the house, it was in need of major restoration. In recognition of the historical significance of the home and as a tribute to Frank D. Lanterman's twenty-eight-year service in the state assembly, the State of California appropriated $500,000 toward the restoration of the home. It was formally dedicated on September 26, 1993, with an impressive ceremony attended by many government officials.

The property is now known as the Lanterman House and was placed on the National Register of Historic Places in 1994. While the Lanterman property is owned by the City of La Cañada Flintridge, it is maintained by

El Retiro (the Retreat) with the family dog in the early days. *Courtesy of the Lanterman Museum Historical Foundation.*

the Lanterman Historical Museum Foundation and is operated as a museum and archives. The Roy Lanterman family never threw anything away, and the archives contain Frank Dexter's music collection and the archives of the La Cañada Historical Society, as well as other community collections that are available for research. The house is open for tours, recitals and features revolving exhibits. It also hosts many local school groups during the year.

7
The Le Mesnager Family and the Stone Barn

The impressive European-style granite Stone Barn with its eighty-one-grapevine vineyard is the heart of the seven-hundred-acre Deukmejian Wilderness Park in the Glendale Annex. This legacy started with George Le Mesnager, an early French immigrant.

George Who?

An ongoing puzzlement in the valley is how to pronounce "Le Mesnager." Actually, the name was originally Mesnager; the "Le" did not appear in official records until the 1900 census. An 1890 newspaper article gave the pronunciation as "Le-Mes-na-shay." A call to the French embassy came up with "Lur-mes-song-jay." This is a modern pronunciation and probably was not how it was pronounced in George's time. I believe the people of nineteenth-century Los Angeles had just as much trouble pronouncing his name as we do today. What is important is that we attempt to pronounce it correctly.

George was born in the Loire Valley in Mayenne, France, in April 1844 or 1850; his birth date fluctuated in official records. He was a very interesting character. His fingers were in many pies, but his claim to fame—serving in World War I in France when he was a senior citizen—overshadowed his other activities and accomplishments, both laudatory and dubious.

By all accounts, he came to Los Angeles in 1866, when he was sixteen or twenty-two years old (depending on which birth year you believe). When the ten-month Franco-Prussian War broke out in 1870, he "rushed" back to France to fight the Germans. Rushing back at that time meant at least a month's travel no matter which route one took. He served, became a color sergeant and returned to Los Angeles in 1871. He was devastated by France's loss to the Germans.

In November 1872, George became a naturalized American citizen but kept dual citizenship. When he traveled to Europe, he traveled under a French passport, and there is no record that he ever applied for an American passport. About 1875, he married Conception Deolara, who was from Spain. They had four children who lived to adulthood: Louis (1876–1957), George Jr. (1882–1950), Louise (1885–1924) and Jeanne (1888–1963).

Conception died on June 10, 1892, leaving George with four children, ages four, seven, ten and sixteen. Louis had been sent to Switzerland at age thirteen for six years, so he was not around at the time of his mother's death. George Jr. was also sent to Switzerland for two years when he was sixteen.

George's chief enterprise for over thirty years was the G.L. Mesnager Company, in which he had a longtime partnership with another Frenchman, Pierre Durancette. All his wineries and properties in Los Angeles were located around the main plaza, which is now Olvera Street. In the 1880s, George and Pierre had a wholesale wine and liquor business, as well as their first winery, Sunny Side Winery, located at Second and Los Angeles Streets. George was very active in the French community and was a prominent figure and speechmaker at various French gatherings. He was also a founding director of a French newspaper.

Hermitage Vineyard

On February 3, 1986, George and Pierre purchased from Dr. Benjamin B. Briggs, the founder of La Crescenta, an agreement allowing them access to the waters of Dunsmore and Cook Canyons and a tract of land in Dunsmore Canyon in Crescenta. This property is located north of the rancho partition and was originally railroad land purchased by James F. Dunsmoor, who sold it to Briggs in 1882. At a 2,330-foot elevation, it was prime wine grape–growing land. George and Pierre immediately started developing a vineyard, calling the property Hermitage Vineyard.

A September 23, 1889 *Pasadena Star Evening News* article noted that George Le Mesnager was growing and harvesting grapes in Crescenta Valley and had (illegible) thousand grapevines. He was also developing vineyard property in Verdugo Canyon.

Bad Times

On May 25, 1893, George and Pierre's wholesale liquor business in Los Angeles was busted in a midnight raid by the Los Angeles tax collectors and the Internal Revenue Department for lapse of liquor license, illicit distilling of brandy and illegal tax stamps. It turns out that they were distilling brandy from Saturday night to Monday morning, and neighbors complained of the light, smoke and noise. All the stock, valued at $100,000, was confiscated. Using an inflation calculator, this works out to over $2,000,000 in 2012 dollars. I believe the figure was exaggerated, but it had to have been a tremendous financial blow.

This obviously caused George and Pierre to go out of business. Three months later, they dissolved their Hermitage Vineyard partnership, and that same month they leased the Deukmejian Vineyard property to another Frenchmen, Albert Rambaud, for a period of seven years starting on October 18, 1893. Albert was interested in growing grain crops and corn, but under the terms of the lease, he was obligated to maintain the vineyard.

On the Rebound

After the bust, when he couldn't get a liquor license anymore, George was appointed a notary public by the governor of California. He had an office in Los Angeles, became a court translator, was an executor of the will of Manuel Leonis of Calabasas and went in the private mortgage business.

On September 6, 1894, he married a thirty-five-year-old Frenchwoman, Marie du Grey. They had one daughter together, Yvonne, born in November 1897. In the same month of his marriage, he transferred ownership of the Dunsmore vineyard property to Marie. There was trouble with the tenant, Albert, and on September 21, 1898, Marie sued Albert for failing to maintain the vineyard, not properly watering it and letting the cistern go dry. Somehow, they patched up their differences, and Albert continued to lease this property.

On January 11, 1900, eight months before the lease was to expire, Marie again sued Albert for the same allegations. Albert said all this had been taken care of in 1896. One interesting detail was that he improperly pruned the vines; he was supposed to leave only three buds, but he left five or six. Whatever the outcome, this property came back under the management of the Mesnager family in 1900.

By this time, oldest son Louis was in charge of all G.L. Mesnager Company businesses and was responsible for the winery, supervising the building of the two-story wine barn starting in 1904 and other structures on the property, as well as a 1915 expansion. Louis was also managing other vineyard properties, as well as grazing sheep on Anacapa Island in the early 1900s. In 1908, George purchased Anacapa Island for $8,000. This was a very shrewd move, as the State of California was planning to open an automated lighthouse on the island. The lighthouse was opened in 1912, and Louis was again leasing land on Anacapa to raise sheep since by this time ownership had passed to the state.

World War I

George Louis Mesnager's main claim to fame is that he was the oldest solider to serve in France in World War I. According to an interview with grandson Louie conducted in 1991 for the Historic and Architectural Survey Report for the Le Mesnager Vineyard Ranch, when George announced to his son Louis that he was going to war, Louis was said to have replied, "But you are too old to fight," whereupon George was said to have responded, "I promised in 1870 to be there if France were invaded again, and I want to keep my promise."

He first went to France in July 1914 and entered the army as a private serving in the 106th Infantry. He was injured at Calonne—thrown fifty feet by a high explosive shell—and was sent back to the States in July 1916 for a furlough. Through the entreaties of the French embassy in Washington, D.C., he returned to France in 1917 and was assigned to the headquarters of General Pershing, serving as a liaison officer for the French army. In March 1919, eight months before the November 1919 Armistice, he returned to the United States. Four months later, his wife Marie and daughter Yvonne went on a visit to France, and

Yvonne stayed. She was married and became a countess but sadly died before 1930.

By 1920, there were no members of the Mesnager family left in Los Angeles. George and Marie were living on Opeechee Way in Glendale, and by 1921 they were living in Verdugo Woodlands, where George owned over 1,300 acres of land (some he sold to William Sparr, and it is now Sparr Heights). Much of this property was purchased from Security Bank in a foreclosure. In 1921, George suffered two strokes; he and Marie went back to France to visit their daughter and to allow him to recover at the family home. He died in Mayenne in September 1923. He had obituaries in the *New York Times*, the *Los Angeles Times* and the *Glendale Evening News*, 95 percent of which concentrated on his World War I record.

Returning from France, George arrived at the Port of New York on March 27, 1919, aboard *La Lorraine*. He first went to Washington, D.C., to deliver papers for General Pershing and then went home to Los Angeles.

George left a large estate, and as a result of his second marriage and multiple titled property ownerships, this resulted in several court battles. The La Crescenta Dunsmore property was not part of the estate, as ownership had already passed to son Louis. The ranch was supported by the sale of water as part of the Mesnager Land and Water Company. In a telephone interview in 1991, grandson Louie Le Mesnager confirmed that the property was entirely supported by income from the sale of water for the period extending from the early 1920s to the late 1950s.

Louis and Family

Louis continued operating the Le Mesnager family businesses, including the La Crescenta vineyard. Prohibition dealt a blow to the grape-producing industry in the area, but people could buy grapes to legally make their own wine. They were also sold as table grapes and as a basis for a brandy fruit drink that was legal. In 1920, the Los Angeles business was closed down, and the cooperage, pumps and much of the winemaking equipment was moved to the Dunsmore property. After Prohibition ended in 1932, the wine and brandy operation was resumed.

The Fire

In 1933, a devastating fire ravaged the foothills, and the winery building was greatly damaged. According to the *Los Angeles Times* of November 24, 1933:

> *The next heaviest property loss was that to the L'Hermitage Mountain Vineyards, Inc. at the head of New York avenue, La Crescenta, the winery building and garage both having been destroyed as well as 20,000 gallons of wine and 1,500 gallons of brandy. The loss was estimated at $25,000.*

The Stone Barn after the November 1933 fire. The darkness on the ground is 20,000 gallons of spilled wine and 1,500 gallons of spilled brandy.

After the November 1933 fire, Louis did not sell out but stayed and rebuilt the wine barn. Instead of rebuilding the entire second floor, he built a mezzanine, establishing living quarters on the second floor that included several bedrooms, a living room, bathrooms and a kitchen. The pitched roofline was changed to the present arched truss system. Louis, his wife Anne and their children moved there permanently in 1937. Louis died in 1957, and his son Louie and his family lived on the property until 1960. While George started the vineyard in 1886, it was his son Louis who built the Stone Barn and maintained the property until his death in 1957. He deserves the credit for building and maintaining the Stone Barn.

Myths

One of the myths regarding the property that was disputed by grandson Louie was that there was an orphanage there, which he states is absolutely not true. But the really big myth is that the bandit Tiburcio Vasquez used the canyon in the period from 1850 to 1870 as a lookout from which he could view any movement on the Crescenta Valley floor. In fact, there was a plaque at the property attesting to this claim to fame. (The plaque was later removed by the City of Glendale.) This theory was credited to Will H. Thrall, who devoted much of his life to researching the life of Vasquez, and was put forth as fact in a historical survey done in 1977 with the purpose of strengthening the historic significance of the property. Historians now generally do not believe there is any validity to the connection with Vasquez.

What's in a Name?

The Dunsmore property and canyon have been referenced by many different names over the years. Dunsmore Canyon was named for an early settler, James F. Dunsmoor, and has been called Dunsmoor, Dunsmuir and now Dunsmore. The Le Mesnager property has been called the Le Mesnager Vineyard, Hermitage Vineyard, Le Mesnager Ranch, Inter-Valley Ranch, Dunsmore Canyon Ranch and now Deukmejian Wilderness Park.

The Annex

Originally, the Dunsmore Canyon was part of Rancho La Cañada and was called Las Flores Canyon. In 1883, the western portion of the rancho was developed by Dr. Benjamin B. Briggs, who renamed the area Crescenta. When a post office was established in 1888, they add the "La" in order to not confuse the town with Crescent City, California. In the early 1950s, the residents of Crescenta Highlands in La Crescenta voted to annex to the city of Glendale in order to ensure a secure water supply. This area is called the Glendale Annex, and while it strangely bisects La Crescenta, it still remains part of the Crescenta Valley, albeit with a Glendale address.

The Wine Barn

According to the historical survey, the original wine barn was a large stone building used as a stable and for the storage of equipment, including wagons, sleds and tack, and during harvest season, it doubled as a bunkhouse for the temporary workers. It had a full second story with a centrally located stairway and three tiered levels with full cement platforms. In addition to these structures, a small workmen's cottage, a blacksmith ship and several small wooden sheds were built, including a worker's cottage.

The vineyard operation was relatively simple. The vines were tended throughout the year by a small group of employees. At the fall harvest, the grapes were picked, placed in sledges that were hauled by mules and taken to the Stone Barn, where they were transferred to wagons and hauled to Los Angeles for processing and bottling under the name "Old Hermitage Vineyard."

Saving the Property

The property was listed on the City of Glendale Register of Historic Resources in 1977. The original entrance to the property was at the top of Dunsmore Avenue but is now located one block east near the top of New York Drive, on Markridge Road. Excerpts from an October 6, 2011 article written by Mike Lawler for the *Crescenta Valley Weekly* outline the purchase of the property by the City of Glendale:

Side of the Stone Barn overlooking the vineyard with the mountains in the background. *Courtesy of the Stonebarn Vineyard Conservancy.*

In the late '60s the family decided to sell the property and initially approached both Glendale and the state to purchase the property for parkland. Neither was interested. The Le Mesnager family was then left to sell Dunsmore Canyon to private parties. Developer Bill Bliss bought the property and formed the Intervalley Ranch Company with the intention of building several hundred homes on the site.

Initial opposition to the large development began in the '70s in the neighborhood below Dunsmore Canyon and gained traction with Glendale. By the early '80s, setbacks in the permit process for the developer, coupled with the City geared up for purchasing the property, resulted in numerous lawsuits and lots of legal maneuvering.

In 1984 an agreement for 5½ million dollars was reached with Intervalley Ranch. The City had little money available for the purchase, but was able to cobble together 3½ million from City and Santa Monica Mountains Conservancy funds and Governor Deukmejian came up with $2,000,000. In 1989 the 702 acre property was purchased by Glendale for use as a park.

Many have conjectured that the name of the park is rather obscure. So many other names come to mind that make more sense—Le Mesnager Park, Dunsmore Canyon Park, Mount Lukens Park, Vineyard Park. But the fact remains that without Governor Deukmejian's personal efforts to secure 2 million dollars for this park purchase, we very likely today would be walking the sidewalks of yet another terraced hillside neighborhood, rather than hiking the verdant trails into the unspoiled wilderness above Dunsmore Canyon.

Stone Barn main entrance, 2012. *Courtesy of the author.*

The 2009 Station fire, the worst in the history of the Angeles National Forest, destroyed much of the foothills, but the fire department made a special effort to save the historic twelve-acre Park Center area around the Stone Barn, as well as a historic oak tree located up the hill from the barn that had survived the 1933 fire and is an important part of the park's heritage.

Besides the wine barn, the Park Center historic area includes an amphitheatre, native plantings, picnic tables, a stone restroom building that was built to match the Stone Barn and great views. We owe a debt to Glendale for preserving the property for us and for future generations.

Stone Barn Vineyard Conservancy

The Crescenta Valley grape-growing tradition is being honored and continued through the Vineyard Conservancy. The conservancy is an offshoot of the Historical Society of the Crescenta Valley, especially set up to maintain the commemorative eighty-one-grapevine vineyard that the city planted as part of the extensive remodel of the park in 2004. The city's Parks Department approached the historical society with a maintenance/programming proposal. The affirmative result was the grape harvest of 2007, the first vintage on this property in over seventy years.

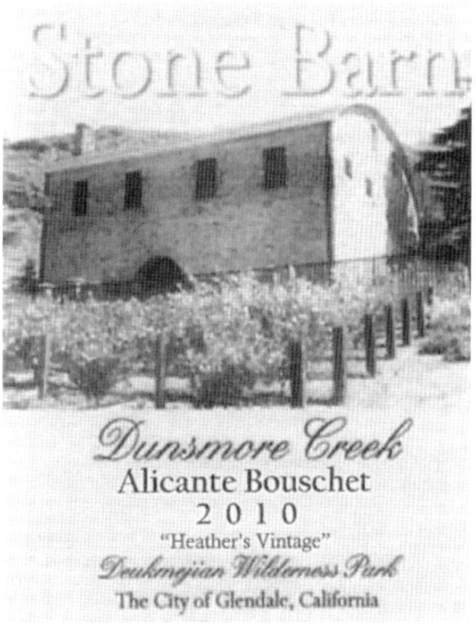

A Dunsmore Creek Alicante Bouschet wine label. *Courtesy of the Stone Barn Vineyard Conservancy.*

The conservancy operates under the direction of Stuart Byles, vice-president of the historical society, his wife Marie Yseta and an active group of volunteers. Activities during the year include trimming, harvesting, grape crushing, bottle washing, bottling, wine tastings, wine classes, field trips and the not-so-romantic task of weeding.

Back of the Stone Barn with vineyard, 2012. *Courtesy of the author.*

Wine grapes planted are Alicante Bouschet and Early Burgundy (a California name, neither early nor a true burgundy), plus Red Flame table grapes; they are bottled under the name Dunsmore Creek.

The official name of the wine barn is Le Mesnager Barn, but it is generally referred to as the Stone Barn, probably because that is easier for us to pronounce. The Le Mesnager family legacy is very much alive in the Crescenta Valley.

8

Theodor Pickens, Fact versus Fiction

Theodor Pickens is generally accepted as being the first "permanent" white settler in the valley. He is also our most maligned historical figure. Why is this? Every drama needs a villain, and he was easy to pick. There are many descendants of early settlers still living in the area, but Pickens left no descendants to offend or defend him, so he is an easy target. One recent history even referred to him as a misanthrope. A misanthrope is a person who hates or distrusts mankind. In all my research on Pickens, I have found nothing to support this, and the record of his life disputes this allegation.

And yes, his name was Theodor, not Theodore. In all early legal documents, this was the way the documents were issued and the way he signed his name. Censuses, newspapers and casual references misspelled his name. In his final will and testament, he was indicated as the more modern "Theodore," but this was only four months before he died, so he just gave in to the misspelling. Either way is correct.

One reason Pickens is so recognized is that his name is still very much with us, in Pickens Canyon, Creek, Wash, Debris Basin, Yard, Park, Tower and Tunnel. He was born in Kentucky on February 21, 1842. Nothing is known of his parents or early life before he came to California. In 1870, Pickens was living in Los Angeles and working on a farm owned by Albert Keschivel, who later became a longtime business partner and one of the witnesses to his land patent application. Keschivel was a farmer, land developer and a well-known published local poet.

This well-known picture of Pickens looks quite informal, but it actually was taken between 1906 to 1911 at the California Portrait Gallery at 61 Colorado Boulevard in Pasadena. Pickens would have been in his late sixties and working in the Arroyo Seco. *Courtesy of the La Cañada Congregational Church.*

Pickens came to the Crescenta Valley around 1871, when he was twenty-nine years old and settled on the lower level of Pickens Canyon. When he found out it was part of the Rancho La Cañada land grant, he moved farther up the canyon and filed a land patent claim with the land office in Los Angeles. After building a cabin and improving the land, he received a land patent for the land in Section 22, which is located north of Briggs Avenue and Shields Avenue. The early settlers could not purchase the land until it had been surveyed by the government, and this was not done until 1877. South of Shields Avenue was Mexican land grant property, which had been surveyed years earlier. The township and Mexican land grant boundaries are shown in Thomas Bros. map books:

> *Name: Theodor Pickens*
> *Date: 30 Nov 1878, Location: CA, Los Angeles*
> *Document #608, Serial#: CACAAA074547, Sale Type: Cash Sale*
> *Meridian or Watershed: SB, Parcel: Township 002N, Range 013W, Section 22*

This was for a quarter of a section, 160 acres, at a cost of $2.50 per acre.

A copy of Pickens's land patent application was acquired from the National Archives in Washington, D.C. His witnesses were A.F. Kerchival, who stated he had known Pickens for eight years, and J.H. Book, who said he knew him for three years. Pickens stated that he settled on the property on January 1, 1873. Improvements to the property were a house, a honey house, two acres of barley and five acres in orchard trees. The quarter section of 160 acres was not square but a very vertical plot.

He was principally a farmer but was also a lifelong apiarist (commercial beekeeper), a partner in Verdugo Heights and, at the end of his life, manager of Teddy's Outpost, an Arroyo Seco mountain resort. He did not sell lumber permits for a living as a recent history stated. In the 1880 census, Pickens was living in the valley, and his occupation was listed as an apiarist.

How Tall Was He?

According to various voter registrations, Pickens was tall (six feet, two and a half inches), had a dark complexion, blue eyes, dark brown hair and a scar on the end of his right third finger. Even for present times, six feet, two and a half inches is tall, but in the nineteenth century, he was a standout. Of the 134 men registered to vote in the 1896 La Cañada Precinct, most men were much shorter; only seven attained the height of six feet. Pickens was, as most people were in those days, slender and mostly likely had a Kentucky accent.

Civil War and Colonels

It has been said that Pickens was in the Civil War and was a colonel. He was twenty-three when the Civil War ended, so he would have been a very young colonel indeed. While there were very young commissioned officers in the Civil War, they were graduates of military colleges. In all my research and in Pickens's obituary, there was never a reference to him being in the Civil War, much less a colonel. The same goes for newspaper references. He is not listed in any of the many extensive Civil War databases, including the National Park Service Soldiers and Sailors and the Pension Indexes.

Most telling is the 1910 census. As 75 percent of Civil War veterans received either a disability or invalid (old age) pension, the federal government wanted to determine exactly how many veterans were still living. A question was added to the census that asked whether they were in the Civil War,

Union or Confederate. In the census, Pickens did not say he was in the Civil War, nor do I believe he ever said he was in the Civil War.

Where did this story start? The very first reference found to the Civil War/colonel story was in a 1953 *Ledger* letter to the editor sent by Charles Pate when he was eighty-one years old. Pate came to the valley in 1893 when he was nineteen years old and settled in La Cañada. He left a valuable photo collection and wrote "Reminiscences of a Tenderfoot" in the 1960s. In the 1953 letter, Pate was defending Pickens and some other early settlers, as a previous article about Frank Lanterman referred to them as "squatters." I believe Pate was trying to pump up the reputations of the early settlers and said Pickens was a colonel for the Union in the Civil War. This letter also contained other inaccuracies about the early settlers.

Pate wrote about Pickens in his later writings, saying he left Kentucky to fight for the Union and was wounded in basic training by a bullet he carried for the rest of his life in his wrist. Have you ever seen a Civil War musket ball? With a bullet in his wrist, he would have been crippled, and the scar would have been noted in the voter registrations. Kentucky was a border state, neutral and had over 170 Union regiments; there would have been no need for Pickens to "go north" to enlist in the Union. None of the references to Pickens serving in the Union ever says what state he enlisted in.

Pate was nineteen when he came to the valley in 1893. Pickens was fifty-one and married with a fifteen-year-old stepson. I doubt if Pickens and Pate "hung out" together. Within a decade, Pickens was divorced and had moved permanently to Pasadena, so how well did Pate know him anyway? Other than very recent histories, no other reference has been found that ever referred to Pickens being called "Colonel" or being a Civil War veteran. Pickens was very good friends with Union colonel Thomas Spencer Hall, so there is no way he could have pulled off such a deception.

As far as the colonel reference, many early settlers were called "Colonel" (or in J.H. Shields's case, "General") as an honorarium, with everyone knowing that they were, in fact, not colonels. Whether anyone actually called Pickens "Colonel" is not known, and he was never referenced that way in any newspaper accounts of the day or in his obituary.

Theo and Ammoretta

Pickens sold the main water rights in Pickens Canyon on January 21, 1878. The following bill of sale is from *Sources of History*:

> *Bill of Sale for Water Rights to Pickens Canyon*
> *$1250. Los Angeles, Cal. Jan 21st 1878*
> *Received of Mrs. A.J. Lanterman, wife of J.L. Lanterman of Los Angeles Co. State of Cal. The sum of Five Hundred and forty two. 00/00 dollars in Gold Coin and one promissory note for ($708.00, Seven hundred and eight dollars—made by said A.J. Lanterman) which when paid will make the full amount of $1250. To be paid me for certain water rights by me. Sold by instrument of (illegible) herewith—to him—*
> *(signed) Theo. Pickens*

Probably the silliest story about Pickens is that he only sold his water rights to Ammoretta Lanterman because she went riding up to his canyon ranch and threatened him with a gun. One can be certain that anyone in those days going into a canyon would be carrying a gun; there were coyotes, bobcats, rattlesnakes, mountain lions and the occasional bear. If she did go up there with a gun, it would have been for protection from critters, not to commit homicide.

Theodor Pickens, at the time, was thirty-six years old and tough as nails and, as June Doughtery would say, "frontier hardened." It would have taken more than short, forty-seven-year-old Ammoretta to cowtow him. While a gun is a great equalizer, if Amoretta had shot off the top of his head or blown off his kneecaps, she would have gone to jail for it. She was upper class, married to a doctor, a Christian and a mother. If Pickens had refused to sell the water rights, would she really have resorted to murder? I think not.

The sale of water rights occurred two months before the March 1878 *Williams v. Lanterman* appeal trial in which several early settlers were called to testify. The entire 176-page trial manuscript is available at the Lanterman House Archives and presents a different picture of the transaction. Most of the testimony is quite tedious and repetitious and focuses on the intent of the partnership, land surveys and whether Williams was trying to buy the water rights from Pickens for himself or for the partnership. According to the testimony, Pickens had a business partner, A.D. Keschival, who was his agent in the negotiations, but in the end he handled it himself.

Pickens's testimony runs several pages. He originally was going to sell the water rights to Williams, but Williams did not have the money at the time. He negotiated with Dr. Lanterman, and they agreed on $1,250 plus forty acres in Section 21. Here is what Pickens testified about selling the water rights:

> *In January, following Lanterman came over and asked me what I would take for my right. I told him I would take $2,500 for all my right and title to the water on the canyon. He didn't say what he wanted with the water nor where he wanted to use it. He told me he was going to run it through the railroad Section 27, and through Government land. He said he didn't know whether they would run it on the grant or not. I told him I would take $2,500. He offered me $1,000. Cash and 40 acres. I was to reserve the water in the Mullaly canyon and lead it into the main canyon. He was to deliver it free on the 40 acres. The 40 acres was in lot 21 on the grant. They were to pay me $2,000. At the end of two years, if I wanted it for that would make it $3,000. in all. Told him I would take $1,250. Cash and the 40 acres. I came down about a week later and sold to Mrs. Lanterman. She paid $455. Cash, the mortgage the doctor had on my place with the interest amounting to about $530. And those 40 acres in lot 21. That was the consideration, I made the papers to Mrs. Lanterman.*

Water gushing in Pickens Canyon in 1908. *Courtesy of Lori Ward Kent.*

So according to the testimony (which was not disputed), he made the arrangements with Jacob Lanterman and came down

In 2012, Pickens Canyon wash is now a concrete channel. *Courtesy of the author.*

to finalize it with Ammoretta. Having his wife purchase the water rights was a very smart move on the part of Jacob Lanterman. The testimony repeatedly stressed that it was her money, her separate money from her father, her wedding money, money that was never part of the marital assets, etc. Thus, the issue of the water rights could not be considered in the trial.

The whole story of Ammoretta threatening Pickens might have started with some good-natured kidding by acquaintances because he sold the water rights to a woman. No one knows how some of these stories come into being. It is a good one but not a true one.

Breaking Up Is Hard to Do

After Delia Dunks's husband died in January 1878, she went into partnership with Pickens in Verdugo Heights, her health resort located off Angeles Crest Highway, north of Vista Del Valle in La Cañada. There were no medical treatments done there, and was more of a boardinghouse than a sanitarium. There is no evidence that Pickens boarded at Verdugo Heights. In the 1880 census, he was not living there. The following excerpt is from *Sources of History*:

> *"Old Feud"*
> *We remember the stories about Theodore Pickens and his partner Mrs. D.W. Dunks. They operated a sanitarium on what is now the Frank P. Doherty place and for some years they got along most amicably with each other. But both were stubborn and most determined. When an argument arose over credit to a houseguest, open warfare broke out. They decided to divide their property—Pickens agreed to move one half of the sanitarium building to his own property to the south. In the meantime, they decided to divide the milk from their Jersey cow. Pickens to milk two teats each day and Mrs. Dunks had the other two. One weekend Pickens took a hunting trip and was gone for two days. The story goes that Mrs. Dunks would not milk the Pickens side of the cow; the poor animal almost died from milk-bag-congestion. When Pickens returned Mrs. Dunks directed him to leave immediately, to move his ½ of the sanitarium building and to remove himself and his belongings.*

With no electrical or plumbing systems, moving a house in the nineteenth century was fairly common, and sometimes a larger house would be cut in half and reassembled at the new site. However, you just don't take half a house; it would make for a very strange roofline. Most likely, Pickens's section was some addition or separate structure on the property. Supposedly, the section that Pickens moved was located at 1117 Green Lane. The current residence at that address was built in 1996.

On December 20, 1882, according to the Los Angeles County Recorder's Office, Book 175, "Theodor Pickens sold to Delia W. Dunks, an undivided ½ interest, in Verdugo Heights including improvements, Section 36. $1000." (The deed is very hard to read; this must have been when they split up their partnership.)

Moving to La Cañada

For a while, Pickens maintained his La Crescenta property while he was in partnership with Delia Dunks in La Cañada. As reported in the September 23, 1882 *Los Angeles Times*, Dr. Benjamin B. Briggs purchased Pickens's 160-acre property in Section 22 for $3,100. At this time, the whole area was still known as La Cañada. Dr. Briggs purchased other land and developed and renamed the area Crescenta, which later became La Crescenta.

A long article about La Canyada in the *Los Angeles Times* of August 5, 1882, included the following item:

> *La Canyada Slope, An Out-of-the-Way Place in the Mountains*
> *Pickens' place on the west side of the slope, recently purchased by Mr. Briggs, furnishes a magnificent view of Verdugo Canyon and mountain, Los Angeles Valley, the low country and the ocean. He says the fog never reaches him in the summer.*

Hunting

Pickens was a well-known hunter and participated in the Hall family annual deer hunting trips during the six-week deer season, and he was frequently mentioned in local newspapers. For example:

> *A California lion was shot by Mr. Theo. Pickens, of Pickens' Canyon, on Wednesday morning. It measured five feet ten inches from the end of its nose to the tip of its tail. [Los Angeles Herald,* April 5, 1878, "Local Brevities"]

> *Tom Hall and Mr. Pickens have gone far back into the mountains on their annual hunting trip after grizzlies and things. [Los Angeles Times,* July 10, 1897, La Cañada]

A group picture most likely taken at the Hall Ranch. Pickens is in the middle.

Love and Marriage

Theodor Pickens was married once and wasn't very good at it. He met and quickly married twice-widowed Electa Carter Rouse in La Cañada on Sunday,

May 29, 1887. They were married by Reverend B.F. Wolfe, a rural Methodist minister assigned to the Monte Vista circuit. The witnesses were La Cañada postmaster Joseph Cockcroft and his wife. Electa had a brother, Julius Munson Carter, who was a Civil War major who lived in Los Angeles at the time and later moved to Pasadena. Electa came to the area in early 1887, as indicated in this excerpt from the *Los Angeles Times* dated April 1, 1887:

> *La Cañada, a Thriving Settlement*
> *Among the new settlers is Mrs. Rowse, from Springfield, Mo., who has bought five acres on the north side of Michigan avenue, on which buildings are being already erected.*

Eleven days before her marriage to Pickens, Electa purchased Lots 1 and 2 of the F.D. Lanterman subdivision of Lot 12 for $2,500. Electa had a nine-year-old son, Paul Rouse; he did not take Pickens's name. Pickens was forty-five, and Electa was forty-two. Their years together seem to have been very productive in farming their properties. They did not combine ownership of their individual land. I refer to this time of Pickens's life as his "respectable period." He is mentioned several times in the newspapers as being a very successful farmer, playing whist with friends, building a fine house in the valley, attending the La Cañada schoolhouse dances, holding an exhibit at the 1892 state fair of cherries in solution and dried prunes and serving on the Republican primary committee.

In the *Los Angeles Times* of November 20, 1890, a general column about La Cañada reported:

> *Among the charming homes in La Cañada may be mentioned those of W.H. McArthur, Dr. Lanterman, Judge Carnahan, Theodore Pickens, D. Williams, son of the late Gen. Williams, and Mr. Ketchum. Col. Hall, an alumnus of Yale college, has a well-cared-for ranch.*

Actually, Pickens's house belonged to his wife at the time, Electa Carter Rouse. It was a showcase located north of Michigan (Foothill) Avenue on the west side of Haskell (now Angeles Highway). It was torn down in the 1960s.

As reported in the *Los Angeles Daily Times* of November 26, 1887, Pickens sued the La Cañada Land and Water Company to enjoin it from laying pipes across his land, and whatever the outcome, when the company incorporated, Pickens was an original director. The *Record-Union* [Sacramento] of August 7, 1891, noted:

Pickens working at his wife Electa's house on the west side of Angeles Crest Highway, north of Foothill Boulevard. Electa and her son Paul are on the front porch. It was one of the finest homes in La Cañada. Circa 1890.

> *New Incorporations*
> *La Cañada Water Company of Los Angeles County*
> *Capital stock, $36,000. Directors—J.L. Lanterman, Theodore Pickens, Ed. Dunham, F.D. Lanterman and R.G. Moses.*

There was a vandalism fire at the La Cañada Schoolhouse, and Pickens testified in the trial, as reported in the *Los Angeles Times* of July 7, 1893:

> *All in Their Bark*
> *How a Man Knew What His Dogs Saw.*
> *Dogs at La Cañada barked loudly on the night of March 16, just previous to the discovery of the fire in the schoolhouse.*
>
> *Theodore Pickens heard them, and others who were in his house at the time also noted the cries of the canines. Mr. Pickens's animals made the noise, and they were not thoroughbreds, neither were they supposed to be endowed with anything more than common dog sense, yet the disturbance they created formed a not unimportant link in the chain of defense set up to clear Lemuel Veflex of the charge of arson yesterday in Department One.*

The case for the people was closed by Deputy District Attorney Conklin just before noon, and then it became evident as to what the cause of the defense would consist of.

Mr. Pickens testified that on the night in question he was playing whist with some friends, when the dogs before mentioned barked loudly. He could tell that they were barking at a human being from the "expression" of their voices, or energy of their cries. They stopped for a time and did not bark until about a quarter of an hour later, when they started in again. This circumstance indicated that someone had passed and repassed the house, going toward and coming from the direction of the schoolhouse. Soon after the bell rang the alarm of fire.

On cross-examination the witness stated that he was quite sure that he could distinguish from the tone of his dogs' barks whether they were barking at a man or other animal.

Pickens was a very successful farmer and was featured in many newspaper articles, as noted in the May 24, 1895 *Los Angeles Times*:

BONANZA IN CHERRIES
The Experience of a La Canyada Fruit-raiser
And another exhibit of cherries from the ranch of Theo Pickens of La Canyada, which, taken with the fruit from Mr. Curtin's orchard, goes far as a convincing argument in favor of the cherry in a profitable fruit for cultivation in southern California. Mr. Pickens claims that he will make more this year from his cherry orchard than he would from an orange orchard of the same size. His faith in the future of cherries raised in this part of the country is sufficient to warrant him in adding six hundred trees to his cherry orchard this spring."

The *Los Angeles Times* of May 25, 1895, printed the following story:

CAN GROW CHERRIES
The Times *has frequently called attention to the erroneous character of an opinion that is widely prevalent among farmers in this section, that cherries cannot be successfully grown in Southern California. At the Chamber of Commerce just now are three exhibits of cherries from three different points.*

The third is from the farm of Theodore Pickens of Canyada, which adjoins Eagle Rock Valley on the north. Mr. Pickens has 900 trees, and considers the crop more profitable than oranges, which may readily be believed, as cherries always bring a high price in Los Angeles."

On August 22, 1895, the *Times* reported, "There was an article regarding the Atlanta Display in the California State Fair Building stating a donation by Theodore Pickens of La Crescenta of orange cling peaches."

On May 29, 1896, the *Times* noted:

> *Cherries Can Be Grown in Southern California*
> *An exhibit sent in to the Chamber of Commerce yesterday amply demonstrates the fact that cherries can be grown in Southern California. In spite of all assertions to the contrary, Theodore Pickens, of La Cañada, shows a quantity of fine Black Tartarian and Royal Anne cherries, taken from eight-year-old trees in his orchard at La Cañada. The trees are breaking down with the weight of the fruit, which is being sold at 12 cents a pound, wholesale rates.*

After nine years, the marriage ended, and the divorce decree, courtesy of the Huntington Library Archives Case #26346, was filed on August 25, 1896. This was a default divorce; Pickens did not contest it. Electa claimed mental suffering, stating that the defendant grievously wounded her feelings, destroyed her peace of mind and, since 1889, was sullen and morose. He drank too much wine and would not speak to her for several days at a time; he swore at her, called her names, shook his fist in her face and, in 1896, threatened to burn down her house and barn and then locked her out of her own house.

Basically, they had two good years. Both newspaper notices of the divorce state the grounds as "failure to provide," but the final decree was indicated on the grounds of mental cruelty. It should be noted that this was before our 1970s no-fault divorce laws, and a specific cause for divorce had to be given—i.e. desertion, adultery, mental cruelty, failure to provide. Electa's testimony had to be quite strong, but regardless, Pickens most likely was a difficult man to live with.

Electa remarried on May 5, 1898, in La Cañada to a much older man, Frederick Snover Crissman, who was Ammoretta Lanterman's brother, and they moved back to Lansing. Electa died on February 20, 1899, in Michigan and is buried in Romeo Cemetery. Her son Paul Rouse moved with her and then married and settled in Detroit. It is not known where Pickens moved after his divorce, but in the 1900 census, he was boarding with Tom and Sam Hall at their Alta Canyada ranch. Pickens was good friends with their father, Thomas Spencer Hall, who died in 1893.

Dad

One of Pickens's nicknames was "Dad," and this has led some people to believe that Pickens had a son, but no record has been found of Pickens ever having any children. In his will and probate, it states three separate times that he had no kin or legal heirs. People who came to the valley after his 1887 marriage might have assumed Electa's son Paul was Pickens's son. T. Fenton Knight wrote the following about Pickens in 1949 in his column, "Early Recollections of La Cañada," in the *La Cañada Valley Sun*: "Mr. and Mrs. Theodore Pickens with their son, Paul, were developing their acreage on the west side of Angeles Crest Highway opposite my father's property, then known as the La Cañada Land and Water Company tract."

Old Heathen

Charles Pate wrote that some called Pickens an "Old Heathen," but he recounts a charming story:

> *Mrs. Waterman, who was a religious woman and a good judge of human nature, has told me that whilst "Dad" had little or no use for churches in general, she could go to him and get a donation, but with strict injunctions that she would not let anyone know that he had given. The reason for this was undoubtedly because "Dad" well knew that her religion was not of the show-window variety.*

While Pickens was not a churchgoer, a minister married him and there was a minister at his funeral. The valley people also referred to the Chinese workers as heathens. It is also interesting that the great majority of original church members in the valley were married women, not their husbands.

Timber!

Probably the worst accusation against Theodor Pickens is that he was somehow responsible for the wiping out of the Big Cone spruce forest northeast of his property in Pickens Canyon in the late 1890s and that this act contributed to the establishment of the San Gabriel Forest Preserve (later Los Angeles National Forest). The preserve was established in 1892, well before the harvesting of the Big Cone spruces. Lumber-harvesting permits were issued after 1892, and many early settlers in the valley obtained them. The lumber patents were issued by the land office in Los Angeles; I have reviewed the original records and timber patent logs that are now in the possession of the Regional National Archives in Perris, California. There is no record of Pickens ever applying for or receiving a timber harvesting permit.

The trees of the San Gabriel Mountains have been extensively harvested from the days of the missions. Loosely based on existing Indian trails, Benjamin Wilson blazed his Mount Wilson Trail for the sole purpose of obtaining timber for his furniture store in Los Angeles. The timber was poor quality, and he quickly discontinued the harvesting. The early French winemakers also tried harvesting local timber to make their wine barrels and found them unsatisfactory and continued to import oak wine barrels from France. The trees were mainly used for fuel in Los Angeles, and the valley residents used the abundant greasewood for their fuel.

While Pickens legally harvested trees on his own property, it wasn't until the Timber and Stone Act of 1878 was passed that massive harvesting of trees on public land was allowed. The act allowed western timberland to be sold for $2.50 per acre in 160-acre blocks. It was supposed to be land that was deemed "unfit for farming" and was sold to those who might want to "timber and stone" (log and mine) on the land. Pickens owned a quarter of Section 22; this section was very desirable for timber harvesting. Will W. Beach, a Los Angeles businessman, had a harvesting permit from 1884 to 1890. Benjamin B. Briggs and Frank D. Lanterman both filed timber claims in this section in 1885, years after Pickens had sold his property to Briggs.

The Big Cone spruce trees in Section 13 were legally harvested by Arthur and Chester Blain in the 1890s under various timber permits they obtained in 1893, 1894, 1896 and 1897. The Blain brothers worked for Joseph Mullally, who owned Mullally Brick Company in Los Angeles. There is a Mullally Canyon that is a narrow canyon tributary in Pickens Canyon and ends at the end of Manistee Drive at the top of Ocean View. Today, it is known as the Mullally Debris Basin.

In *Sources of History*, there is a reprint of a 1953 *Ledger* article about the Big Cone spruce forest. There is no mention of Theodor Pickens cutting down the trees, only the Blain brothers. A trestle system was built to haul the logs that went down to the Briggs barn. There is a 1900 picture of the trestle in Winifred Bathey's photo album entitled "Blain's railway."

La Crescenta: Images of America also gives a correct account of the timber harvesting:

> *This photograph of a waterfall in Pickens Canyon was taken over 100 years ago from the train trestle that crossed Mullally Canyon. In the early 1880s, the growing city of Los Angeles needed fuel for its burgeoning industries. Mr. Mullally (Joseph) of the Mullally Brick Company and his foremen, the Blain brothers, filed timber claims to the east of Pickens Canyon. At that time, the canyons were heavily forested with Big Cone Douglas fir trees, many four to five feet in diameter. A rail tramway was installed, and each summer a crew of Chinese felled the trees, cutting them into four-foot lengths, which they stacked on a small railcar. With one man on the brakes, the car rolled down the rails to Briggs' barn, where the wood was loaded on wagons for the trip to the downtown brick kilns. It wasn't long before the timber supplies were exhausted. The rail line was abandoned, but later used by the Bathey children as a thrill ride with their own homemade railcar.*

Sometimes when you have places named after you, like Pickens Canyon, you get blamed for everything bad that happens there!

MOVING TO PASADENA

Pickens's good friend Tom Hall was married in 1904, and this ended Tom's very socially active bachelor's life. Right after his marriage, Tom's brother Sam sold Tom most of his property and moved to Pasadena. About this time, Pickens also moved to the Arroyo Seco, where he worked at the mountain resorts as a teamster, eventually ending up as camp manager at Teddy's Outpost, a popular tourist camp near the start of the Arroyo Seco trail. While there were cabins for lodging, it was a popular day-trip destination.

GOODBYE TO DADDY PICKENS

Pickens was a caretaker at Teddy's Outpost when he took ill and entered Glendale Sanitarium and Hospital on June 7, 1923. Dr. Roy Lanterman was his personal physician and visited him every day. On June 25, 1923, Pickens

Teddy's Outpost in the Arroyo Seco, where Pickens was manager, circa 1915. Could that be Pickens's Model T Ford? *Courtesy John W. Robinson.*

was transferred to Los Angeles General Hospital, where he died on July 11, 1923. The cause of death was heart disease. He was eighty-two years old. His monument at Mountain View Cemetery in Altadena is engraved with the very affectionate name "Daddy Pickens." He was taken care of by the people of Teddy's Outpost; in fact, the owner, Theodore Syvertson, paid for Pickens's hospital stay at Glendale Sanitarium. The *Pasadena Star News* of July 12, 1923, reported:

> *Theodore Pickens, a pioneer of La Cañada and Arroyo Seco since about 1871, and a native of Kentucky, passed away yesterday afternoon at a Los Angeles hospital.*
>
> *Funeral services will be held tomorrow morning at 10 o'clock at the chapel of Reynolds & Eberle, corner of Fair Oaks and Union. Interment will follow in Mountain View Cemetery.*

According to the Los Angeles Hall of Records Archives, Probate Case No. 63348, 1923, he left an estate of $943.90 consisting of:

The Pickens monument at Mountain View Cemetery in Altadena, with the very affectionate inscription "Daddy Pickens." *Courtesy of the author.*

> *Cash on hand $778.89*
> *1 Ford automobile*
> *1 Gold watch, Hampden make 21 jewels*
> *1 30-30 Marlian rifle*
> *A 2' Ivory Rule* [this could not be found after he died]
> *2 hives of bees and 1 honey separator*

After all his final costs were taken care of and his estate settled, the net was left to the Benevolent Order of the Elks, Pasadena Lodge 672, with the instructions that the interest therefrom be used for charitable and hospital purposes. Pickens's good friend Sam Hall was an active member of this lodge and its piano player for many years. While Pickens was not a member of the lodge, he would have gone there as a guest of Sam Hall.

Charles Pate wrote quite favorably about Pickens in his memoirs:

> *Those who knew him best realized what an honest & independent man he was. In spite of a curious temper, some of which may perhaps* [have] *been due to a sensitiveness which sometimes caused him to imagine a slight when none was intended, he was a genial companion & was missed by all of us when he passed on.*

So what do we know about Theo Pickens? He was tall, a hard worker and honest. He had friends, was a farmer and a lifelong beekeeper and did not involve himself in land speculation, nor did he ever have or sell timber permits. He did not cut down the Big Cone spruce trees; he wasn't very good at marriage, and he had several nicknames. He died respected and had people who cared enough about him to inscribe his monument with "Daddy Pickens."

9
The Elusive General Shields

In La Crescenta, we have Shields Canyon, Shields Debris Basin and, at the top of Briggs Avenue, Shields Street. They were named after an early settler who was referred to as "General Shields." If General Shields were living today, I believe that he would be in the Witness Protection Program, as researching him has been extremely difficult.

Like many men in the nineteenth century, Shields did not go by his first name, only his initials, "J.H." Shields. In a 1953 letter to the editor of a local newspaper, Charles Pate, a chronicler of valley history, referred to Shields as Confederate general James Shields. Pate was a latecomer to the valley (1893, at age nineteen), and much of his information was second- or third-hand and written when Pate was in his eighties. Researching James Shields was a dead-end.

Finally, a research trip to the Southern California Genealogical Library in Burbank led to the 1884 Los Angeles County Voter Registration, and there he was, living in La Crescenta as John Howard Shields, not James! A check of the Los Angeles County Land Patents also revealed that John Howard Shields was awarded a land patent in La Crescenta Section 22 on December 5, 1890. Now the search started anew with the correct name.

I found that our J.H. Shields was born in Sevier County, Tennessee. His parents were Samuel and Eliza Shields, first cousins, both from old southern families. According to *Notable Southern Families* by James P. French (vol. 1, 1918):

> *They had a son, John Howard Shields, who was born September 15, 1929 in Sevier County, Tennessee. He married Margaret Amanda McMillan, daughter of Andrew McMillan and Mary Littleford.*
>
> *They had eight children, namely, Ella B. Shields, deceased, Lizie I. Shields, deceased, Samuel Shields, deceased, Mary C. Shields, who resides in Los Angeles, Alexander McMillan Shields, who resides in San Francisco, Margaret Lea Shields, who resides in Los Angeles, William Shields, who resides in Mentone, California and Lawrence Shields, who is in the Medical Department of the United States Army.*
>
> *Margaret McMillian Shields died in Cincinnati, Ohio, August 6, 1900. Her husband, John Howard Shields, died near Jalapa, Mexico, March 17, 1902.*

While John was born in Sevier County, the family settled in Grainger County, Tennessee. In the 1850 census, John was at home; he was twenty and listed his occupation as a merchant. His father, Samuel, was a physician and most likely also a gentleman farmer. According to a separate slave census, Samuel had nine slaves ranging in age from five to thirty-seven. John Shields's younger siblings included Mary W., Ann E., Samuel E., Elizabeth A. and Alonzo. Shields married Margaret Amanda McMillan on January 15, 1852, and they had eight children, not all of whom lived to adulthood. In 1860, John and Margaret and three of their children were living near Knoxville, Tennessee, where he was a farmer. In 1870, they were in Rockville, Alabama, where he was again a farmer.

Indian, Mexican-American and Civil Wars

The legend is that Shields was a Civil War general from Tennessee. Well, that is pretty easy to check. The Civil War was documented from day one; every small town, county and state kept track of their veterans, and reunions were held even before the war ended. There are many sources, including the National Park Service Sailors and Soldiers database, as well as local sources and many copyright-free books available online—and there is no Shields in any of them. The Tennessee State Library has a card file for all Tennessee men who served in the Civil War, and Shields is again missing from these records.

No Confederate general John Howard Shields is found. There was only one John Howard Shields from Tennessee who served in the Civil War, and he was discharged as a lieutenant. A copy of this Shields's pension file from the Tennessee State Library indicates that this was not our John Howard Shields, as he never left Tennessee. This Shields's wife died during the Civil War, he never remarried and had no children.

Perhaps our Shields was in the Indian Wars? There is no John H. Shields in the *Index to Volunteer Soldiers in Indian Wars and Disturbances, 1815–1858* (National Historical Publishing Company, 1994).

Perhaps he was in the Mexican-American War? A review of *Mexican War Veterans: A Complete Roster of the Regular and Volunteer Troops in the War between the United States and Mexico, from 1846 to 1848* (A.J. Witherbee & Co., 1887) revealed no John Howard Shields. This was a compilation of officers. The Tennessee State Library also has files on all Tennesseans, officers and enlisted men—again, Shields is not listed.

Moving West

After living in Alabama in 1870, the Shieldses moved to Ohio, where one of their sons, Lawrence, was born in October 1872. By 1874, they were living in Los Angeles, where Shields was mentioned in newspaper articles and advertisements. In the 1880 census, Shields and his family were living in the Vernon and Florence Road District; he was a farmer. The family consisted of Shields, fifty; Margaret, forty-seven; Mary C., eighteen; Alexander, fifteen; Anna M., eleven (born in Tennessee); William A., ten (born in Alabama); and Destovin (Lawrence), seven (born in Ohio).

In 1874, Shields was involved in several large land transactions in Santa Barbara and Los Angeles. He was an officer of the Centinela Land Company of Los Angeles and was one of the managers of the sale of the Redondo and Centinela Ranchos consisting of twenty-five thousand acres. Shields was very involved in local interests and belonged to the Horticultural Society, where he was often a speaker. He also wrote articles for Los Angeles newspapers regarding agricultural and railroad issues. He was an extremely successful farmer and businessman.

According to the January 3, 1878 *Los Angeles Herald*:

> *The attention of dairymen and those having horses to pasture is directed to the advertisement of J.H. Shields, which appears elsewhere. General Shields, in addition to having the biggest pumpkin ranch on the coast, has*

> *extensive alfalfa pasture fields which he offers at reasonable rates to those desirous of putting animals out to pasture.*

A January 11, 1878 narrative about Los Angeles in the *Los Angeles Herald* had this to say about Shields:

> *Leaving the San Gabriel valley and passing over to the Compton and Florence region, on the Wilmington branch of the Southern Pacific Railroad, we enter upon the "artesian belt." There are now in the vicinity of Compton, between two and three hundred artesian wells. Besides these, there are several flowing wells at Florence, near which place is the farm and residence of Gen. Shields. But as we did not intend this to be a lengthy letter, I will forbear dilating upon the General's 350 acres of squashes, yielding 3,000 tons, planted at a cost of $1,200 and sold for $6,000. leaving a net profit of $4,800.*

Moving to La Crescenta

According to Shields's land patent application, he moved to his La Crescenta property in July 1882. Right after that, he became ill. According to the August 3, 1882 *Los Angeles Times*, "The friends of General J.H. Shields will regret to learn of his serious illness from typhoid fever."

On September 1, 1882, the *Times* reported, "General J.H. Shields has so far recovered from his recent illness as to be able to go up toward the mountains for a change of air."

Like many early settlers, in order to acquire land under the Homestead Act or, in the case of valley pioneers, under the Land Act of 1820, they were supposed to live on their property full time. The realities of life prevented this, and many stayed in Los Angeles attending to jobs and interests while developing their foothill properties.

Land Patent Application No. 1029

Shields's land patent application, a copy of which has been obtained from the National Archives in Washington, D.C., provides a wealth of information, mainly because his family did not live with him and he had to prove that he did, in fact, live on the property full time. His original filing of a land patent was on May 23, 1882. His witnesses to the final application, dated April 26, 1889, were B.B. Briggs, George Englehardt, J.H. Bemis and C.T. Bathey. The legal description of the property was: "N ½ of NW ¼ of SW ¼ and Lot 1, Section 22, 2 N, 13 W, S.B.M." It consisted of 134.46 acres.

Shields's house was described as a timber frame with a shake roof, three rooms up and down, one door and three windows. It was already on the property and had been built by Lewis H. Price. Since this was government land, Price must have originally filed a land patent claim on it but subsequently abandoned it, allowing Shields to file his claim. It is estimated that over 50 percent of land patent applications were abandoned. Shields paid $2.50 per acre for the property.

Englehardt said that the house was twenty by twenty feet, Dr. Briggs said ten by fifteen and Shields said it was twelve feet square. Whatever its actual dimensions, it was a very small cabin. Shields stated that his family visited in 1882 and 1883 "but not so often of late [1889]." He claimed his family did not live there because it was too far from town, and there was no school. He cultivated about five acres in apples, corn and vegetables.

La Boca del Shields Cañon

Shields Canyon.

Shields's ranch was located at the top of La Crescenta Avenue. He kept track of the rainfall at his ranch for the *Los Angeles Daily Times*, the *Los Angeles Herald* and the *Pacific Rural Press*. In his reports, the ranch was always referred to as La Boca del Shields Cañon, which translates to "The Mouth of the Canyon Shields."

La Boca del Shields Cañon (The Mouth of Shields Canyon). Located at the top of Pine Cone Road, the entrance now filled in with debris basin fill.

Life in the Valley

Helen Haskell, a niece of Dr. Benjamin Briggs who married Seymour Thomas and settled in La Crescenta, wrote about her time in the valley in the mid-1880s, when she was young and lived there with her mother, Maria Briggs Haskell. In an interview published in the March 4, 1938 *Crescenta Valley Ledger*, she wrote about Shields:

> *How well I remember General Shields, straight as an arrow—riding horseback through the valley. He was over 70 and looked only forty. His receipt for eternal youth was no worries; no business cares, sleeping with his head out of a window and a diet of raw graham flour and apple sauce. It worked in his case. (Oh, if we could all follow it!) His family lived in Los Angeles and relieved him of all cares.*

At the time, Shields was about fifty-seven, not seventy, and three of his children were still quite young. His youngest was only nine years old when Shields moved to the valley. While it was nice for him that he was relieved of all cares, he left his wife and young children without the benefit of the emotional support of a husband and father, not exactly something to be proud of. One can understand his wife's reasons for not moving to the valley—it was very isolated, with no churches, social activities, medical facilities or schools for the children, and to move into a one-room cabin with several children would not be very desirable. She was from a prominent southern family and probably did not relish, at age fifty and as a mother of eight, starting all over with a frontier life. If Shields had really wanted his family to visit for extended periods of time, especially during school vacations, he would have built a bigger house instead of being content to live in a squatter's cabin.

He was a small-time farmer; five acres is not a big endeavor. In his newspaper articles, he always signed his name J.H. Shields, never "General." It was other people who referred to him as General. He was one of the nine founding members of the La Crescenta Presbyterian Church, one of only two men. He was very social and liked to give speeches at local events. He was a great booster of the Crescenta Valley and was very active in the (unsuccessful) effort to bring the railroad to the valley. The following article was printed in the *Los Angeles Daily Times* on September 7, 1883:

> *KEEPING QUALITIES OF LOS ANGELES FRUIT*
> *Gen. J.H. Shields, who is at present residing on his ranch at La Cañada, sent in town yesterday four apples which score another point for the keeping qualities of the Southern California climate. Three of the apples were of the crop of 1882 and were picked from the tree one year ago. The other is of the crop of 1883, just gathered from the tree before it was sent into town. As might well be expected, the apples of last year have rather a withered and cheerless expression, and resemble the countenance of Egyptian mummies in their general appearance; yet had they not been disturbed, might have kept until the opening of the new year. The General's method of keeping his apples is to place them in shallow boxes in a cool cellar; and treated in this manner, all of his fruit kept remarkable well this year. The climate of the section has not seemed well adapted to keeping the deciduous fruits, but it is evident that, with proper treatment, they will do as well, or better here than elsewhere.*

On September 1, 1887, the following was reported in the *Los Angeles Herald*:

> *CRESCENTA CAÑADA FRUIT*
> *The* Herald *acknowledges the receipt of some choice fruit raised by Gen. J.H. Shields of Crescenta Cañada. It consists of a specimen of*

late Crawford peaches, another a second crop of early York peaches and a cluster of sixteen white figs. Heretofore the fig trees of Mr. Shields have borne but three figs to the cluster, but this year he practiced pruning of about six inches from the ends of the limbs and was rewarded with an immense increase of fruit. His hale early peaches have produced two crops and his apple trees, now loaded with fruit, are blooming for a second crop. The fruit is very fine, in fact it is in the class superlative, and shows that Crescenta Canada is one of the finest localities in the state. The General attributes the production of two crops to the fact that the trees are so far removed from surface water, with its attendant coolness, that the warm soil stimulates continued growth and production of fruit. It may be that the warm uplands will make deciduous fruit trees into evergreens. Quinces have already become evergreen in such localities, and apples seem to be half changed already.

Other Properties

The ranch property was not the only property that Shields owned in the valley; it was only 134 acres. The July 3, 1888 *Los Angeles Daily Times*

Shields Canyon Debris Basin. The debris basins were put in after the horrific flood of 1934.

reported a transaction for eighty acres: "H.B. Briggs to J.H. Shields, E ½ of NE ¼ of Section 21, T2N, range 13W. $3000."

There are many different stories about who, what and when Shields sold his properties, but researching this would require a year at the County Recorder's Office in Norwalk. The ranch property was sold to Samuel Merrill, who later sold it to Harvey Bissell of vacuum cleaner fame, and he named the property Hi-Up Ranch.

Leaving the United States

In 1895, at age sixty-five and well enough to travel, Shields applied for a passport to travel out of the country for two years. The passport provides some interesting facts, confirming his birth date and place of birth and stating his occupation as a lawyer! His physical description was six feet tall with a high forehead, blue eyes, a straight and prominent nose, a small mouth, a round chin, brown hair, a light complexion and a long face. The application states that he intended to return to the United States within two years. He stated that the passport was to be sent to General John H. Shields at a San Francisco address. This is the only time I have found Shields referring to himself as a general. Perhaps it gave him some gravitas in his business dealings. At the time, his son Alexander was living in San Francisco.

Margaret died in Cincinnati, Ohio, on August 6, 1900. She had been living there with two daughters, Mary and (Margaret) Lea. The Cincinnati Main Library could not locate an obituary for Margaret. Mary and Lea eventually moved back to Los Angeles and died there in 1949 and 1950, respectively, never marrying. Son Lawrence was a physician who served in World War I in France and settled in Ohio.

Shields died near Jalapa, Mexico, on March 12, 1902, and is most likely buried there. Jalapa (Xalapa) is the capital of the state of Veracruz. What he was doing in Mexico is anyone's guess. A final adventure, perhaps? Much of Shields's life story remains elusive. He certainly was not a general, and I do not believe anyone thought he was a general. These kinds of honorifics were quite common in the nineteenth century. There is no record that he was in any military endeavors. He was an early settler, a so-so father and a great supporter of the valley—and his name lives on.

10

Adolphus W. Williams and the Founding of La Cañada

Adolphus W. Williams, along with Jacob L. Lanterman, a neighbor in Lansing, Michigan, founded and developed Rancho La Cañada. Williams, feeble, with his health ruined by the Civil War, wanted to settle in a more hospitable, healthy climate. He was born on May 11, 1830, in Rochester, New York, to John Chester and Charlotte Fitch Williams. By 1850, he was in Lansing, Michigan, where he earned a living as a jeweler. On December 23, 1852, he married Mary Crosby Baker, and they had five children: Adella, Charles F., James Chester, Adolphus Wesley Jr. and Justus H. Williams.

Mary Crosby Baker Williams, picture taken in Pasadena. *Courtesy of L.K. Shackelford.*

The Civil War

With a wife and four children at home, Williams enlisted in the Union army on April 25, 1861, for three years and was commissioned as a major. He was a citizen soldier, not a career military man or a graduate of a military academy. A descendant, Richard W. Williams, recounts that Adolphus's family had a long military history. His maternal grandfather, Elijah Fitch, was a veteran of the War of 1812. His great-grandfather, John Chester Williams, was a Revolutionary War officer, and his father, John C. Williams, was involved in the Canadian Patriot War in 1838 as an American. His father was on the losing side, and he spent about eight years in prison, mostly at a Tasmanian (Australian) penal colony.

Williams was promoted to lieutenant colonel on March 6, 1862, and assumed command of the Twentieth Michigan Infantry a month after promotion to full colonel on July 26, 1862. The Twentieth Michigan Infantry Regiment was always engaged on the front lines, never on duty in the rear. The Twentieth took an active part in the Maryland (Antietam) and Virginia (Fredericksburg) campaigns.

Colonel Williams in his Civil War uniform. *Courtesy of Richard W. Williams.*

The regiment is reported to have lost more commissioned officers killed in action and from wounds than any other Michigan regiment. More than 11 percent of its enlisted men were killed in battle or died of wounds. In the great "battle summer" of 1864, the regiment lost more men killed and wounded in action than the total number it had bearing arms at the opening of the war. Colonel Williams was wounded three times, on April 15, 1862, at Yorktown, on May 5, 1862, and on May 31, 1862, at Fair Oaks.

Williams received a discharge on November 21, 1863, and was awarded a disability pension; his disability papers have been shared and recount a horrific series of illnesses and injuries. He contracted typhoid fever in the Peninsula campaign and had relapses. He was wounded at Fair Oaks and rendered deaf in his left ear at the Battle of Yorktown due to shells bursting overhead. He suffered from the common complaint of dysentery, and the records list eleven different times that he was treated for this debilitating disorder. They state that after his discharge, he was unable to work or perform any manual labor.

After his discharge, he was promoted to brigadier general brevet, U.S. Volunteers, on March 13, 1865. In the nineteenth-century U.S. Army, brevet promotions were extremely common. During the Civil War, approximately 75 percent of all senior officers received one form of brevet or another, particularly during the final months of the war or after their discharge. While he had been brevetted to a general in the Volunteers almost two years after he resigned his commission, Williams actually served as a colonel in the Twentieth Michigan Infantry regular army.

Rancho de la Barrancas/Rancho of the Canyon/Rancho La Cañada

In 1875, Williams came to the valley, staying at Delia Dunks's Verdugo Heights resort and exploring options to settle in the area. He was joined by Dr. Jacob L. Lanterman, a dentist and fellow Lansing resident. He moved permanently to the valley in September 1875. On December 16, 1875, Williams and Lanterman purchased Rancho La Cañada from A.B. Chapman and Andrew Glassel, originally a Mexican land grant carved out of a larger Spanish land grant, Rancho San Rafael. It was composed of 5,832 acres. They reportedly paid $10,000, a bargain even in those days. To visualize how much land this is, our nearby Griffith Park is only 4,310 acres. It was only after they had purchased the property that they realized that most of the water rights had already been acquired by the early valley settlers. The search for water and the need for accurate surveys delayed their plans to develop their lots.

As the rancho was Mexican grant land and not public land, it had not been surveyed by the federal government. Surveying the property was done sporadically, and there were disputes over the surveying and a lawsuit ensued. Jacob Lanterman sued Williams to expedite the surveying of the property. Williams won in superior court, and that trial manuscript no longer exists.

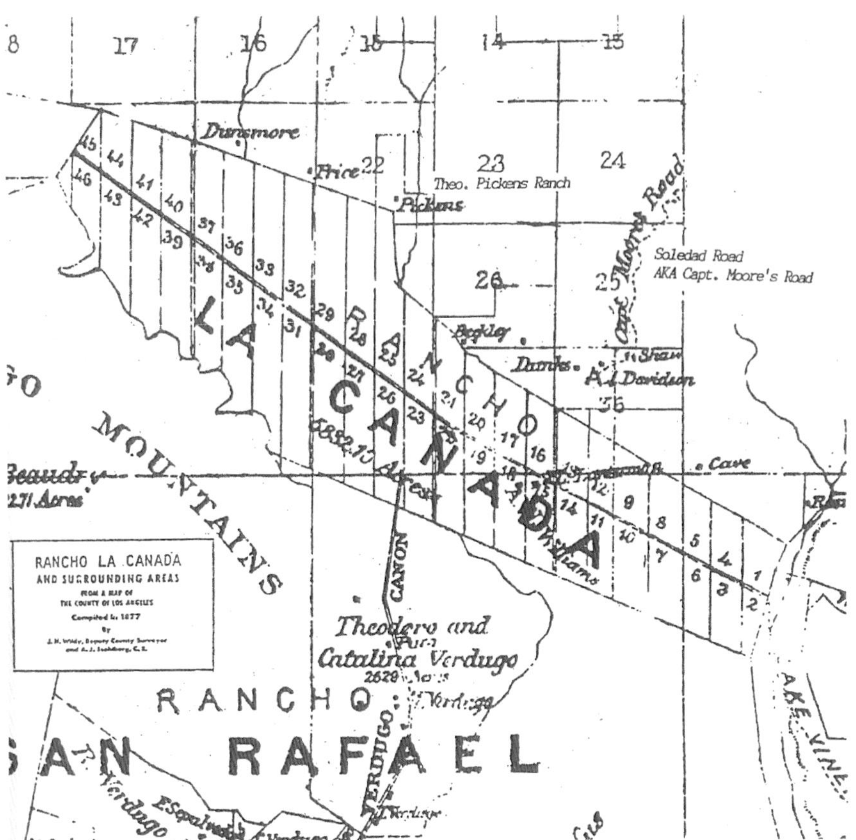

This La Cañada subdivision map shows how Rancho La Cañada was divided into forty-eight one-hundred-acre lots.

Lanterman appealed the verdict, and the January 1879 178-page California Supreme Court Appeals Trial manuscript is available for viewing at the Lanterman Historical Museum Foundation in La Cañada Flintridge. The transcript is repetitive and tedious but provides valuable information about the valley, as several local residents were called as witnesses.

Lanterman won the appeal. The final outcome was that Jacob Lanterman got ownership of the odd-numbered lots and Williams the even-numbered lots on either side of Michigan Avenue (Foothill Boulevard). The forty-eight one-hundred-acre lots were numbered odd/even, so they both owned lots on either side of the street. An extensive account of the trial and witnesses' statements starts on page 103 of June Dougherty's *Sources of History*. Williams's residence was on Lot 18 and Jacob Lanterman's was on Lot 15, both located south of Michigan Avenue next to each other.

While the trial was in process, Williams died on March 12, 1879, at the age of forty-nine from chronic illness and wound complications. According to the *Los Angeles Herald* of March 13, 1879:

> *WILLIAMS—At his residence, La Cañada March 12th, Col. A.W. Williams, aged 49 years and 10 months. The funeral will take place from his late residence, at 11: A.M. to-day. Friends and acquaintances are invited to attend without further notice.*

It has been stated that Williams died of tuberculosis, but no death record for him has been found. Since Williams was originally buried on his ranch property, his death may not have been formally recorded, as a burial permit was not needed. When Mountain View Cemetery in Altadena was established in 1882, his remains were moved there and constituted the thirteenth interment in the new cemetery. He is buried in a family plot with a tall pyramid monument that has a Masonic symbol on it. It incorrectly gives his age as fifty-two years. There is also a small Civil War marker that was placed later by a Civil War organization. On one side of the pyramid there is a missive:

> *In my father's house are many mansions*
> *I go to prepare a place for you*

The Huntington Library Archives in San Marino are saving and archiving Los Angeles County Court Records that are over one hundred years old. A review of Williams's probate file consisting of thirty-four separate documents was done at the Huntington. There were two minor children (Adolphus and Justus) at the time of Williams's death, resulting in trustees being appointed for the minors and numerous court rulings. It took several years to settle the estate. The probate file gives a good picture of property values and costs in 1879:

> *Probate Case #1150, Los Angeles County, California*
> *Last Will and Testament dated August 26, 1878*
> *In the Name of God, Amen*
> *I, Adolphus Wesley Williams of La Cañada, County of Los Angeles, State of California, of the age of forty-eight years.*
> *First—Humbly grateful for the numbers of Mercies granted me during my past Life, by the great Jehovah and humbly asking his blessing upon this act, and upon the Dear ones herein named:*

Mary C. Williams—all personal property, Life Insurance, Homestead—Lot 18—La Cañada, Lot 6, Lot 8
Adella C., Ketchum—House and Lot No. 6, Block 150, City Lansing, Michigan, 40 acres, Lot 16, La Cañada, CA
The west 20 acres of Lot 16, is dedicated school, church and cemetery purpose.
Son Charles Fremont Williams, Lots 4, 12, 46, La Cañada
Son James Chester Williams, Lots 2, 20, 44, La Cañada
Son Adolphus Wesley Williams, Lots 10, 30, 40, La Cañada
Justus H. Williams, after death of his mother, the Homestead viz Lot 18 and at majority Lots 14 and 24, La Cañada
Disposal at will of Lots 22, 32, 34, 36, 38 and 42, La Cañada
Witnesses to the will—John C. Hay, Section 35, Jacob M. Youngling, Section 36
Property Appraisal dated July 24, 1879
$8633. debts do not exceed $2000., estate is solvent
2 horses—$50
1 double buggy—$75
1 set double harness—$10
1 cow—$25
1 plow—$10
1 drag—$10
Household furniture—$100
Allowance for widow and minor children—$40. per month
Expenses
Funeral—$55
Attorney fees Lanterman vs. William trial—$350
Allowance to family—$1000
Attorney fee and expenses—$300
Executors—Mary C. Williams, Adella C, Ketchum, Chester (James) Williams

The attorney for the Williams family was Will D. Gould, a Los Angeles attorney who owned properties in La Cañada and for whom Gould Avenue is named. The final petition for the Lanterman and the Williams family rancho property was granted on March 31, 1881. The probate closed on June 12, 1885. Mary Williams had been awarded her husband's Civil War pension, and she eventually moved to Pasadena.

The Homestead property was located south of Foothill Boulevard (Michigan Avenue) at Cornishon Avenue, where the Lanterman Auditorium

The Williams Homestead residence on Cornishon Avenue below Michigan Avenue (Foothill Boulevard) around 1880. The house was torn down after 1949 to make way for the Lanterman Auditorium. *Courtesy of L.K. Shackelford.*

The Adolphus and Mary Williams pyramid monument in the family plot at Mountain View Cemetery in Altadena. *Courtesy of Paula Hinkel.*

now stands. Mrs. Williams sold the Homestead, including water rights, to Adoniriam J. Sanborn on July 15, 1884, for $6,500. Mary Williams died on May 29, 1905, and is buried in the Williams family plot at Mountain View Cemetery. There are Williams descendants in California but none known to be living in the Crescenta Valley.

If Adolphus W. Williams had not died so soon after coming to the valley, he surely would have been one of the major figures in the long-term development of La Cañada. This was reflected in his bequest of the western twenty acres of Lot 16 to be dedicated to school, church and cemetery purposes.

Bibliography

If you steal from one author it's plagiarism; if you steal from many, it's research.
—Wilson Mizner

Burdette, Robert B. *Greater Los Angeles & Southern California: Portraits & Personal Memorandum*. Chicago: The Lewis Publishing Company, 1910.

Dougherty, June. *Sources of History La Crescenta*. La Crescenta, CA: self-published, 1993.

Farnsworth, R.W. *A Southern California Paradise in the Suburbs of Los Angeles: Being a Historic and Descriptive Account of Pasadena, San Gabriel, Sierra Madre, and La Cañada*. Pasadena, CA: R.W. Farnsworth, 1883.

French, James Preston. *Notable Southern Families*. Vol. 1. Chattanooga, TN: The Lookout Publishing Co., 1918.

Harrel, Al. *History of Valley Water Company*. La Canada Flintridge, CA: self-published, 1977.

Hathaway & Associates. *Historic and Architectural Historic Survey for the Le Mesnager Vineyard Ranch*. Crestline, CA, 1991.

Hunt, Roger D. *Colonels in Blue: New York Union Army Colonels of the Civil War*. Atglen, PA: Schifter Publishing, 2003.

Jackson, Helen Hunt. Diary Manuscripts. Colorado College Tuft Library.

Kennedy, Irene Ward. *Family History of Ward, Briggs, and Allied Lines*. Burbank, CA: Malan Industries, 1962.

La Cañada Presbyterian Church. *The First Hundred Years*. La Cañada, CA, 1985.

Lawler, Mike, and Robert Newcombe. *The Crescenta Valley: Images of America*. Charleston, SC: Arcadia Press, 2010.

———. *La Crescenta: Images of America*. Charleston, SC: Arcadia Press, 2005.

Lombard, Sarah R. *Rancho Tujunga: A History of Sunland/Tujunga California*. Los Angeles: Bridge Publishing, 1990.

Mazen, Don. *The History of La Cañada Flintridge*. La Canada Flintridge, CA: self-published, 2003.

McGroaty, John Steven. *History of Los Angeles County*. Vol. 3. Washington, D.C.: American Historical Company, 1925.

Montrose-Verdugo City Chamber of Commerce. *Montrose, California The First Eighty Years*. Montrose, CA: in-house publication of the chamber of commerce, 1993.

Newcombe, John. *Rancho La Cañada*. DVD, 2007.

New York State Civil War Units. http://localhistory.morrisville.edu/sites/unitinfo/hall-92.html.

Oberbeck, Grace J. "A History of La Crescenta and La Cañada Valleys." *Ledger*, 1938.

Pate, Charles. "Reminiscences of a Tenderfoot." Manuscript at the Lanterman Historical Museum Foundation, n.d.

Pinney, Joyce Y. *A Pasadena Chronology, 1769–1977*. Pasadena Public Library, 1978.

Pomeroy, Elizabeth. *Lost and Found Historic Landmarks of the San Gabriel Valley*. Pasadena, CA: Many Moons Press, 2000.

Robarts, William Hugh. *Mexican War Veterans: A Complete Roster.* Washington, D.C.: A.S. Witherbee & Co., 1887.

Robinson, John W. *Trails of the Angeles*. Berkeley, CA: Wilderness Press, 2008.

Robinson, W.W. *The Forest and the People: The Story of The Angeles National Forest.* Los Angeles: Title Insurance & Trust Company, 1946.

Schechter, Kenneth A. *Lanterman House Dedication Book*. La Canada Flintridge, CA: Lanterman House Museum Historical Foundation, 1998.

Taylor, Mathew F., and Jasper N. Searles. *History of the First Regiment Minnesota Volunteers*. Stillwater, MN: Stillwater Press, 1916.

Index

D

E

F

G

H

J

K

L

M

O

P

R

S

T

V

W

Y

About the Author

Jo Anne Sadler started doing family history research in the late 1970s and has always been interested in local history and the lives of what some consider "ordinary" people. She has written family history and research articles since the 1980s and has given and/or participated in several presentations in recent years about people who lived in the Crescenta Valley. A Minnesota native, she has resided in the Glendale area for over thirty-five years.